Simplified Success

5 Keys to an Amazing Life

Enjoy your successful journey!

Mark Ledford

Simplified Success

5 Keys to an Amazing Life

By
Mark Ledford

Foreword by:
Dale Calvert

Edited by:
Dawn Calvert
Barbara G. Lyons

Copyright © 2020 by Mark Ledford

FIRST EDITION

All rights reserved. No part of this book may be used or reproduced by any means, graphic, electronic, or mechanical, including photocopying, recording, taping or by any information storage retrieval system without the written permission of the author/publisher except in the case of brief quotations embodied in critical articles and reviews.

ISBN: 978-1-7349207-0-3

Design/Printing by:
Right Eye Graphics
311 Henry Clay Blvd.
Ashland, Kentucky 41101
(606) 393-4197
righteyegraphics.com

Dedication

This book is dedicated to my wife, Christy. Your love, wisdom and support has given me the freedom to carry through with this book. I am so blessed to have you in my life and thank God for allowing us to continue this amazing journey as one. I love you and look forward to what He has planned for us in the next chapters of our life together.

Also, to our daughter, Micah. You are an amazing young lady charming everyone with your beautiful, carefree spirit. My prayer is for you to experience the wonderful joy of marriage as your mom and I have; that God will direct your path and you will take your shot at life by following the passions He has placed in your heart. I love you and look forward to seeing your destiny unfold.

And ultimately, I dedicate this book to God, who gave me the outline and inspired this writing. Thank you for your guidance and for opening the doors to get this book into the hands of those who need it. Your will be done.

> "Many times, you find a book that speaks to one generation or about one facet of life. What you find in Simplified Success: 5 Keys to an Amazing Life, is a book that crosses multiple generations and speaks to all facets of life. The author writes from personal experiences but also goes beyond these experiences, landing truths in the heart of every reader. This book will give you the building blocks to a better life and the knowledge to become the best you."
> **—PATRICK LAGER, Pastor, International Evangelist & Area President, Whitaker Bank**

> "Simplified Success: 5 Keys to an Amazing Life" is an insightful, self-improvement book that outlines how young people can overcome life's obstacles and increase success through simple, effective tips. This well-written book provides anyone with the uncovered secrets of a successful life. My entire career has been spent preparing young men and women for life's journey. This book guides them through this journey."
> **—EDWARD C. STEPANCHUK II, LTC (Ret), U.S. Army, High School Senior Army Instructor**

> "In his book, Simplified Success, Mark Ledford shares with his readers in a concise yet thorough manner "Five Keys to an Amazing Life." Having known Mark for over 40 years, I am comfortable in saying that much of his success has come from what he now writes. As a grandparent of four, I will see that each grandchild receives a copy of this book. No one is too young to be taught these principles, nor too old to begin living them."
> **—DAVID POINTS, Retired High School Principal, Administrator & Coach**

Table of Contents

Foreword 9
Introduction...11

CHAPTER ONE:

Social Skills for the Real World

The Importance of Humility: Yes Sir / No Ma'am 13
Introductions: Meet and Greet 15
Conversation: Dialogue — "Throwing the Ball Back" 17
Develop a Network 19
Group / One-On-One Involvement 21
Cell Phone Etiquette..24

CHAPTER TWO:

Financial Health – Making Money Work for You

Part I

Using Simple Math (without a calculator).............................27
Living within Your Means 29
Balancing Your Checkbook 30
Compounding Interest from the Borrowing Side 35
Managing Credit Cards 36
Financing an Automobile 38
Buying Your First Home 41

Part II

Compounding Interest from the Savings Side 53
Compounding Interest Chart 54
Saving for Retirement..57
Budgeting 59

CHAPTER THREE:

Job Preparation – Make a Great First Impression by Being Prepared

Online Classes 69
Trade / Vocational School 70
Community / Technical Colleges 71
Colleges and Universities..74
Financial Aid 76
Scholarships..79
Cover Letter and Resume 80
The Prelude to the Interview 86
The Interview: Greeting, Keys to a Successful Interview 89

CHAPTER FOUR:

Physical Health – You Only Get One Shot

The Importance of a Healthy Diet....................................93
Healthy Snacks — Fruits, Vegetables and Nuts..............94
Breakfast Foods and Main Courses 95
Moderation is the Key..97
Exercise 98
Drink Water 99
Tobacco, Drugs and Alcohol..100

CHAPTER FIVE:

Spiritual Health – Your Eternity Depends Upon It

Forgiveness and Salvation 107
Prayer and Meditation 109
Drink from Good Books, Especially the Bible................115
How to Read the Bible 116
Going to Church 118

Final Thoughts 120
My Prayer for You..122
Special Acknowledgments 123
About the Author...126

Foreword

I have a little sister, one sister for that matter. She is incredibly special, and if I could search the world and find a perfect husband for her, he would be someone who would love, honor, cherish and respect her. Someone who would treat all members of our family like his own.

Looking back over the last 30+ years since Mark Ledford married my sister Christy, he would not only become the perfect mate for her, but someone who I would grow to love like a brother. He would become someone who I could laugh and cry with and have countless stimulating, thought-provoking conversations. He is someone who has prayed with me and for me more times than I can count. Frankly, it's hard for me to even imagine our family without Mark.

If you know Mark Ledford, you like him. It seems wherever he goes, Mark is continually running into and talking to people he knows. He's the kind of guy who never meets a stranger. He shows no favoritism and treats everyone with the same respect, kindness, and openness.

Those who know Mark on a deeper level, know what a man of impeccable character he is, that he is the greatest friend you could ever have, and you have incredible respect for his business acumen. You love him for who he is as a Christian, husband, dad and human being.

FOREWORD

I operate a personal development seminar company. I give a speech called "Balanced Living", and every time I have the opportunity to provide this presentation to an organization, the person I think about who exemplifies the concept of balanced living is Mark.

Simplified Success is a masterful work that could have only been written by Mark Ledford. Mark doesn't just talk the talk. For over 30 years, I have witnessed him live and breathe the concepts he writes about in this book.

Simplified Success is the perfect gift for graduating seniors in your life. For that matter, it should be part of the curriculum and required learning before a student is eligible to graduate. The sound advice Mark offers in this book is something from which every young person can benefit. If you read this book and give a copy to someone else, you would do your part in making the world a better place.

If you are in mid-life or are an honored senior citizen, *Simplified Success* will speak to you. Sometimes the paths to success are so simple and so clear we see right through them; Mark gives you the roadmap in this book. My hope is that you will internalize the concepts and implement them in your life. Knowledge without action leads to self-delusion. Enjoy *Simplified Success*, apply the principles in your life, and share them with others.

—Dale Calvert

Introduction

Life is a journey, and we all want to do it well. We have dreams and desires and our own thoughts on how to achieve these goals. This book lays out some very practical and sound fundamental principles that will help you achieve the things you want out of life.

We all know that life is tough. Life is even tougher if you don't have the basic skills needed to get ahead and stay ahead in today's world.

We have seen the morals and values of our society slowly fade away over the years. Grandparents, mentors and others who set the example for us have since passed and we are only left with what they taught us. Many young people nowadays have never had these mentors in their lives, and frankly, some don't even know they need help. They have never been taught how to handle basic situations, how to carry on a conversation, how to balance a checkbook, how to eat nutritionally, and so on.

By knowing some basic fundamentals, you will be able to not only survive but to thrive in today's world. You don't have to be Albert Einstein to get ahead in this world and to have a wonderful life. You only need sound, basic, fundamental principles to achieve respect, financial security, spiritual wellness, and good health.

INTRODUCTION

If everyone knew a little about and applied most of what is covered in this book, happiness would increase, incomes would increase, and crime would drop. Following these principles consistently will increase your chances of living a happy and successful life.

I hope you enjoy this book and can implement these fundamentals so you can enjoy your life to the fullest and pass these life lessons on to your children and those you mentor.

CHAPTER ONE:

Social Skills for the Real World

The Importance of Humility: Yes Sir / No Ma'am

"Yes sir - No ma'am." These words used to be quite common in our society. Not only were they expected, but more likely, they were required. Whether it was the local postal worker, shoe clerk, custodian, or bank president, it was "Yes sir and No ma'am!" These words show an element of respect, basically stating, "I understand that you are older than I, and perhaps have more wisdom than I, and have been doing life longer than I have. Therefore, I am going to give you the respect that you deserve." Not only does this attitude show respect, it also humbles us.

Humility is not an exciting word in today's culture, however, it is a trait that all of us need to keep in check. We all have eaten humble pie and not one of us likes the taste! However, it is necessary to have a slice every now and then so we don't become arrogant and think we know it all. If you think you know it all, most people don't want to hear anything you have to say.

There are two ways to be humbled; choose to humble yourself or be humbled by others. It will happen one way or the other, and you get to choose. By humbling yourself, you are stating that you don't know it all and realize you have more to learn. Being humbled in public is embarrassing and something most of us don't care to experience.

To be humble is to show respect. Showing respect for our elders is not only the right thing to do, it's the smart thing to do. Showing respect helps open doors and can be the one thing that gets you that job or promotion you've been seeking. Using this one principle on a consistent basis throughout life will take you places and provide opportunities that you would not have had otherwise. It's as simple as that. Apply basic principles of respect consistently, and over time you will enjoy the success you're looking for.

As our mentors, World War II Veterans, and grandparents, fade away, we are only left with memories and the values they taught us. If you are a parent or grandparent reading this, you know what I am talking about. You may have already instilled these and many other positive life lessons into your children over the years. If so, you have seen the rewards of those lessons manifested in them.

If you are a young person reading this, you may or may not have been taught how to respect others and how to show humility. Begin to practice these traits. Think about situations where you can apply these basic skills then watch

CHAPTER ONE

yourself and those around you change!

Showing humility and being respectful to others creates good habits and opens doors and opportunities for you.

Introductions: Meet and Greet

Introducing someone to another person is becoming a lost art. Sure, it's still done, but fewer and fewer introductions are done to ensure success. I realize this is the 21st century and some things have changed, however, respect for both parties involved hasn't. Both parties should know each other's first and last names, then, you want to find some common ground so each person can make a connection with the other. The party who is making the introduction (this is you) will be the one to follow through on trying to find this common ground.

This scenario has happened many times for me at the bank, but one clear example comes to mind. One morning a friend of mine, Bob Butler, came to the bank to see me. As we sat in my office, Bob told me what he needed and then asked whom he should see. I knew immediately he needed to speak with Kelli Wise, one of our Customer Service Representatives (CSR). As Bob and I walked toward Kelli's office, I was thinking of how to make a connection for each of them. I wanted to find common ground that would be the catalyst for a nice conversation. During that ten second walk to Kelli's office, what I needed to say came to me.

The introduction went like this: "Kelli, I want to

SIMPLIFIED SUCCESS

introduce you to Bob Butler. Bob, this is Kelli Wise, our CSR. Kelli, Bob played football for the University of Kentucky, and Bob, Kelli was a cheerleader for the Cats!" I could see the expression on both of their faces, and I knew immediately a bond was created. The connection for them was that they both had participated in sports at the University of Kentucky. Not only did this introduction set the tone for a nice conversation, but it established mutual respect and admiration.

Knowing each of them enabled me to create an automatic connection of common interest revealing an interest of one that matched the other. Common ground is an exceptionally good ice breaker and the catalyst to other pleasant conversations. This not only paved the way for a successful business deal, it was also the beginning of a new relationship, which almost guaranteed Bob would come back again.

There are many business situations where this scenario may be helpful. Business owners and employees who rely on people to buy their goods and services must be "people" people. They must be people who like people and want the best for each person with whom they come in contact. The owner's or employee's goal is to make his or her customers feel special and to help them connect with others through common ground.

I am a banker, and I love people. I grew up in the same, small town where I have enjoyed my 34-year career. This is an advantage for me because I know many people in our small county.

I love getting to know each person and his/her

CHAPTER ONE

interests. In my business, I have enjoyed some great relationships and have had the opportunity to introduce hundreds of people to others.

Banking is a relationship business. Some of the folks who come to the bank come to see me, trusting I will direct them to the best person to help with their need. The key is to listen to your customer's need and introduce him/her to the right person, while finding common ground both can build on.

Much of business is about relationships and connecting with people. The more people you know and know well, the greater the opportunity to attract and keep good business. Helping create a conversation between two people is an art form that cannot be overlooked.

Conversation: Dialogue — "Throwing the Ball Back"

Another social skill that seems to be lacking is the art of dialogue in a conversation. We've all seen too many conversations where one person is doing all the work; the person who is asking all the questions! These one-way-street conversations are no fun and don't last long. My mother compared the dialogue in a conversation to playing catch. She said to have good conversation each party must "throw the ball back." What she meant by this was that each party should participate by not only answering questions but *asking* them as well. This back and forth dialogue allows each party to engage with the other, thereby benefiting both. It's like playing catch but doing so with conversation.

SIMPLIFIED SUCCESS

It's best to ask open-ended questions that require more than a yes or no answer from the other party. Here are two examples of the same question asked in different ways. "Do you like school?" The obvious answers are yes or no. The same question asked in an open-ended way would be: "What about school do you like?" Now, the receiver of the question can say what he/she likes about school. Open-ended questions provide the means for good dialogue.

This back and forth dialogue takes different twists and turns and helps you learn more about the person with whom you are speaking. It also gives you an idea if you will continue to pursue a relationship with this person after the conversation has ended. If the person with whom you are talking is not good at "throwing the ball back," try another question and then find an opportunity to interject your side of the conversation. This is also a good opportunity for you to lead the conversation toward something you may need. For example, you may find out through a conversation and by asking questions that this person works for the college you are considering or at the company to which you have applied for a job. Not only is back and forth dialogue interesting, it can also be very beneficial.

You never know when a conversation may lead you to a certain college scholarship you have had your eye on or a job that could set you up for the rest of your life.

All it takes is a little effort and getting outside your comfort zone. By making the effort to get outside your comfort zone to make the conversation a good one for both parties, you have created an introduction to possibly much

CHAPTER ONE

more. Once a conversation is started, it can take many different paths. You don't know where the conversation will lead. Your next conversation could be the one to set you on your path to prosperity. It just takes some interaction and interest in the other person. Otherwise, the conversation will end without any chance of continuing the relationship, along with possible opportunities that will be lost forever.

While my family and I were at Disney World last year, we were standing in a line waiting for the next adventure ride. It was one of the more popular rides that year, so we waited in a long line! While we were waiting, a couple and their young daughter were in front of us. She was dressed in her Halloween costume and we commented on how cute she was. Of course, they appreciated the comment and we struck up a conversation. During the conversation, I found that the dad and I had a mutual interest - fishing. He mentioned that he and several of his old high school buddies rent an RV and go to Montana for stream fishing once a year. I shared some of my fishing stories, and we both enjoyed a pleasant conversation. I found out where he and his group went and thought this would be a great trip to take with some of my friends.

Conversation opens your eyes to so many adventures and possible networking opportunities.

Develop a Network

Developing a network, in my opinion, means to connect with people, to have acquaintances, and to see them often enough for you to be on their minds. Pursuing conversation is not only a courteous and pleasant thing to do, it also gives you more opportunities to learn new things from others. This will help you achieve the goals you have set and the successes you desire. How much you socialize and network with others is up to you. Your only limitation is your desire to strike up a conversation with the person next to you. Obviously, this comes more naturally to some than others.

We are all created by God and each is created uniquely, which means we all have different personalities. Some of us are extroverts and require relationships and interaction while others are introverts and covet alone time. There is nothing wrong with either – it's just the way we are wired.

Extroverts tend to be able to mix it up with others and look forward to social activities. Extroverts are the life of the party. They are the ones who bounce from person to person, smiling, shaking hands, and loving every minute of conversation. These types get their energy from people. They are good at small talk, serious talk, and all talk in between. When the party is over, they are the ones trying to convince everyone the party has just begun! Well, that might be a little overboard, but you get my point. Extroverts have no trouble carrying on conversations with most people, therefore, they must be careful not to say the wrong things. They must guard their words. Saying the wrong thing is much worse than saying nothing at all. This is the extrovert's greatest challenge - saying too much! This can kill a friendship or a deal more quickly than anything.

Introverts, on the other hand are more reserved. They are likely the ones who would prefer to stay at home, read a

CHAPTER ONE

book, and wind down after the workday. Introverts tend to get their energy from being alone. They may choose to avoid social situations as these require intermingling with people, sometimes for hours. Inevitably, introverts will find themselves at these functions or parties from time to time and they need to know how to make the most of these situations. It's more difficult for introverts to get out of their comfort zone, so it will take some effort to arrive at the enjoyment stage. In social situations, introverts must be selective with whom they have conversations and not spend much time with people who will physically drain them. If they are in a conversation and know that it's not going anywhere, they must politely excuse themselves and find someone else to talk with. At some point, they will find the person with whom they have common ground. That person will cause them to be relaxed, and it's then they have found *their* conversation and the person with whom they have begun a relationship. Not only has the introvert found a new friend, they have opened themselves up to a whole set of new people with whom they may be able to network. By surveying the situation, and the group, and by carefully seeking out those with whom they may be compatible, they will be able to not only endure the situation but possibly make a friend and/or connection that could last a lifetime.

Both the introvert and the extrovert must have a good balance of interaction, conversation, and relaxation in their lives. While the extrovert may spend 65% of her time with people and still be ready to interact, the introvert may need 65% of alone time to recharge his batteries. All of us have some of each characteristic, but most of us will favor one or the other. It's important that you recognize this not only in yourself but also in others, especially your mate. When you know how to recognize this characteristic it will help you understand when he says, "Let's go." But until that time, whether you are an introvert or extrovert, give a conversation your best shot because you never know where it may lead.

Mixing it up, getting to know people, enjoying conversation; these actions will take you places and afford you opportunities that you would have never had by keeping quiet.

Group / One-On-One Involvement

We all need interaction with people. Relationships make the world go around. We cannot do life without people, nor should we. God placed us on this earth to be His instruments. We all have talents, which should be used not only to help ourselves and our family but to help others in need. These needs can come in any form of physical, emotional, or spiritual, therefore, it is important to know what our strongest attributes are and use these talents to help others.

Before you get involved with a group, do a self-assessment. Find an area that appeals to you, then pursue a group, charity or activity that goes along with your interest. Search your heart - what is your passion? What gets you excited? What can you not stop thinking about? Okay guys, I know where you are going with this, but seriously, passion is the key to life. Passion gives you purpose and excitement that, when acted upon, satisfies your deepest, innermost desires. When you have passion, you can do anything you set your mind

CHAPTER ONE

to. Once you have found what it is that excites you, find a way to channel your interest into helping others. If you enjoy sports and kids, volunteer to coach a Little League baseball team. You don't have to be the head coach, just volunteer and be a part of a team and make a difference in a youngster's life. Do you enjoy cooking? Find a local soup kitchen or group that makes meals and delivers to the shut-in and homeless. Do you enjoy math, history, French or another subject that you excelled in at school? Help tutor a student through your local school program and make a difference. Work with your church's youth group; read to kids at an elementary school. Find something you enjoy and pursue it! Do an internet search on your categories of interest and type in the word "volunteer;" you will find enough volunteer work for the rest of your life! If the group or activity requires a long-term commitment, decide whether you can commit. Only commit long-term to those things you genuinely care about; those things for which you have a passion.

Passion is the key that will allow you to be most effective in a group or one-on-one setting. You may ask, "How do I know what my passion is?" Your passion may be so deep inside you that you are not sure what your passion is. Start thinking back to when you were younger. Think about those things that stirred you. This is a start. What did you want to be when you grew up? Were you able to fulfill that dream or are you still trying? If not, is that passion still inside you? Thinking about your interests, your love of something really gets your motor running again and helps set your path for helping others and yourself. God placed passion inside all of us. Passion is a gift from Him and how we use it is our gift back to Him.

All of us have talents, and we are all different. We can use our talents individually or come together collectively to utilize our talents for the good of others. We can be good by ourselves and sometimes we can do more with two or three others around us. Collective ideas, support and camaraderie are worth the effort of working as a group. A group also helps refine the social skills we all need to be successful in life. Life is so much more fun with people in it. Life is so much more rewarding when you are doing something you love and helping someone in the process.

Get involved passionately – it's what makes life worth living!

Cell Phone Etiquette

The cell phone - what a tremendous innovation. We carry the world in the palm of our hands! Every bit of information you would ever need and want is right there ready for you to indulge. Yes, it is captivating; all the things it can do and all the places you can go and see. The texting, internet surfing, the use of apps and social media can be so addictive that some people are on their devices up to 18 hours per day. Some people have been so "into" their phones that they have walked into oncoming traffic and been hit by cars. Many have died this way. No social rules come with cell phones. It's there, we buy and begin using. We sink our minds into its endless array of information and off we go to

CHAPTER ONE

wherever we want - head down, thumbs getting stronger and stronger by the day. Sometimes we get so focused on our device and what it can do for us that we forget everything and everyone else around us. We pay no attention to anyone who is trying to talk with us. If an acknowledgment is made, it's a quick "uh-huh" or "yes" or "no", but nothing more. There is no attempt to carry on a conversation. Once the person trying to initiate the conversation sees that you have no intention of looking up from your beloved communication device, he or she turns you off and goes in a different direction. This is not only sad but rude by the one using the cell phone.

We still have social etiquette in this world, and the cell phone must conform to its rules. My daughter Micah is 18 years old, and like 95% of today's youth, has a cell phone. It is an extension of her body. She is attached to it like we men are attached to our wallets. She enjoys it immensely and would like to take it everywhere she goes. We have allowed this most of the time, but there are times when a cell phone is not appropriate. One is at the dinner table. My wife, Christy, and I enjoy eating most of our meals around our kitchen table with Micah. It is a good time to find out how school is going, how her friends are doing, and about the new developments in the high school musical that she participates in each year. The phone is not welcome at our table. This gives us a chance to have some uninterrupted conversation for 20 minutes and pour into our daughter instead of her pouring into the device she enjoys so much. This not only gives her a break from the endless chatter and social activity, but also allows her to work on the art of conversation.

SIMPLIFIED SUCCESS

Mastering the ability to converse is becoming a lost art as the older generation passes on. We must work to create opportunities that were once so commonplace but are now few and far between. The brief moments that we have to practice the art of conversation, in between cell phone tweets and texts, must be quality moments.

We, as parents, must make conversation a part of our family life. The habit of dialogue helps our children gain confidence and broadens their horizons. Having meaningful conversation daily helps them develop their conversation skills. This gives them the confidence to go out into the world and meet interesting people and take advantage of endless opportunities.

Remember, a conversation never started is an opportunity lost forever!

CHAPTER TWO:

Financial Health — Making Money Work for You
Part I

Using Simple Math (without a calculator)

    Personal finance is a subject some people don't like to think about because they think it's too hard to understand. These folks go through life buying the usual big-ticket items they must have, like the car and the house, but never put much thought into the path they are taking regarding their financial future. Most of their work is spent figuring out *what* car to buy or *what* house to purchase. In this chapter, I will attempt to give you some clear direction on how much to buy and how to finance it. Knowing a few simple facts can save you time, money, and energy. Someone once told me that you must work *smarter* instead of *harder* to get ahead financially. There is no truer statement made when it comes to making your money work for you!

    It's a fact that many people don't like math, but it's also a fact that you had better be decent at it or you will end up

SIMPLIFIED SUCCESS

paying a dear price financially in the long run. I'm not talking about algebra, trigonometry, or calculus. The topic here is general math; the kind of math you use or need to use every day of your life - addition, subtraction, multiplication, division, fractions, percentages and decimals.

Multiplication tables that were once pounded into our heads as kids are now tossed to the side in favor of computers and calculators. Kids and adults alike pick up their cell phones to calculate the simplest of equations. Ask most people if they have seen a store clerk struggle making change when the cash register has malfunctioned, and they will most likely answer "Yes."

"Okay," you ask, "Why do I need to know math when I have a calculator ready and waiting?" Doing the math in your mind activates brain cells. Doing mental exercises keeps you sharp, keeps your mind alert and when you're alert, you are better able to field questions and handle circumstances as they arise. To stay sharp, you need to find ways to hone your math skills. To do this, you must know the different ways numbers are expressed.

Fractions, decimals and percentages are all related to one another. They are simply different ways of stating the same number. For example: ¼ is .25 or 25%, one-fourth or a quarter. Here a number is expressed as a fraction, decimal, percentage and in word form. These figures, numbers and words are used in many different forms and in many different situations every day of your life. Numbers are a big part of your daily activity, so the more you know about the forms these numbers can take, the better off you'll be in understanding numerical life and what goes on in it.

Many of us like to go shopping and buy things we need and want, and we all desire to save money while doing it. Stores

CHAPTER TWO: PART I

are crowded with people looking for the best bargains; store sales are happening at every corner and the fun begins! You enter one of your favorite stores, and you see tags and sale markers that scream "35% off" or "60% savings", whatever the case may be. You're excited to find an area that draws you in. You browse, and finally, an item catches your eye; it's on sale! Now you want to figure how much your new treasure will cost you. You look at the price and you look at the sales percentage, but it just doesn't compute. This is where many people cannot figure out how much the item is going to cost; they're not sure how to calculate the discount on the item. When you know simple multiplication and subtraction, you can do this in a matter of seconds. This is where your multiplication tables, knowledge of decimals and subtraction come in handy.

Let's say you see an item that has a price of $60 and it's 60% off. The easiest way to do this is to multiply 60 x .60 (Hint: 6x6), which equals 36. This is your discount. Now, this is where the subtraction part comes in. Subtract the $36 from $60, and you have a sale price of $24.00 for the item you want to buy.

It's fun to be able to walk through a store and glance at items and sale percentage tags and be able to determine quickly what the sale price is for that item. The idea behind this is to get you thinking about money and mathematics and how you can use these tools to make better choices in other financial areas of your life.

Living Within Your Means

The number one theme you will find in this chapter revolves around *living within your means*. "Living within your means" is simply spending less money than you bring in. This sounds easy enough but there are plenty of subtle ways you can fall into the trap of overspending. You will discover several strategies that will help you decide on actions to take regarding your personal finances.

Here are six main points I want you to get from this chapter:

1) Spend less money than you make
2) Reduce your interest cost and fee cost
3) Spend less on large purchases
4) Reduce debt quickly
5) Save consistently
6) Make wise financial choices

You have choices and the ability to dictate your financial future! You can choose to manage your money wisely or you can choose to be careless and let it slip through your fingers. The choice is yours.

Balancing Your Checkbook

Billions of dollars a year are made by financial institutions from many people who do not balance or reconcile their checking accounts. When an account is not managed properly, errors are more likely to occur, and these errors can be costly. Shareholders and employees of financial institutions want their customers to be successful in managing their money. These men and women care about their customers and have an array of products to help them succeed. But, as much as they desire this success for their customers, their customers must first learn to help themselves.

CHAPTER TWO: PART I

Consider this scenario:

You visit a bank and open your account. The Customer Service Representative (CSR) explains the various deposit accounts the bank has to offer and you choose the account that is best suited for your needs. You are now the proud owner of a debit card, box of checks, deposit slips, and a checkbook register. The CSR's explanation of the process continues: "This is your checkbook register. Make sure you add any deposit and subtract any withdrawal from your account so you know how much money you have left." You are now on your own to navigate the dangerous waters of checkbook management.

The checking account is a wonderful product offered by financial institutions everywhere. If your account is managed and handled responsibly, it can be an account with no fees. Many institutions call this "Free Checking." However, an account not managed carefully (even a Free Checking account) can be very costly. The cost of the account ultimately depends on how well you manage it.

Checkbook management is not taught consistently in most public schools. Many adults don't balance their own bank accounts, so they haven't taught their children. The truth is, if you don't learn to do this on your own or through a personal finance book, chances are you'll have to learn the lesson the hard way, the expensive way. But the good news is - balancing your checkbook is not hard. It only takes a minute a day or five minutes a week. It doesn't have to be done daily or weekly, but it must be done at least monthly and done right, or you will pay a heavy price for what we call returned or "bounced" checks.

The charge for a check written or point-of-sale

SIMPLIFIED SUCCESS

transaction on an account with insufficient funds averages $36.00 **per transaction**. You have heard of bounced checks. This means the check you wrote or debit card transaction you initiated at the retail store was presented to your bank to be paid from your checking account. However, your account did not have enough money in it to cover the item you purchased. The banker now has a decision to make. She can pay your transaction even though your account has no money in it, or she can return the transaction back to the merchant where you bought your item. Either way, you are charged the $36.00 fee which is promptly subtracted from your *negative* balance, and the bad news gets worse. The bank sends you an overdraft notice by mail or email, but snail mail is slow, and email sometimes doesn't get opened. What happens if you have already initiated four additional transactions? You now have five insufficient transactions to deal with.

    As you can see, this gets very serious, very quickly! In this example, you notice the problem after five transactions have tried to post. The total fee cost to you is $180.00, which is promptly deducted from your already *overdrawn* account. If this isn't bad enough, it gets even worse. If these items are not paid by your financial institution, they are returned to the merchants, who then *charge additional fees* of $25-50 per item because they have been inconvenienced. So, if you bought a gallon of milk for $3.00 and didn't have the money in your account, this gallon of milk could ultimately cost you $89.00 ($3+36+50)! Think about it this way. A person earning $9.00 per hour *would have to work nearly 10 hours* to *cover the purchase of one gallon of milk!* To cover the five transactions mentioned would take nearly two week's pay! Wow, that hurts!

    This overdrawn account example plays out in every

CHAPTER TWO: PART I

financial institution in the world daily. Most financial institutions have overdraft protection programs which can help you work through this issue, but these services are not free. Don't put yourself in this inconvenient situation. Take responsibility and commit to making the choices that will help you keep more money in your pocket; *log all transactions in your register daily and balance your checkbook on a regular basis.*

Now, here's the good news. One minute each day can help you avoid this financial issue. Most banks have very convenient websites, enabling you to manage your account very easily online, so make sure you do it. It's simple addition and subtraction. Once you break the ice and do it several times, you'll find a good system that works for you and become more comfortable with it as you go.

Managing your checking account is time well spent and can save you thousands of dollars over the course of your lifetime. You can use an elaborate Excel spreadsheet if you choose, but I prefer to do it the old-fashioned way, entering the transaction manually each time I make a withdrawal or deposit. It doesn't need to be fancy; it just needs to be done and how you do it is up to you. On the next page is an example of a manual checkbook register with a few entries.

Starting from the top and far left, the register begins with the *check number*. From there you can keep things organized with *date, transaction description, payment amount, checkmark* (which is a box to mark if the check has "cleared" meaning the transaction has been deducted from your account balance), *fee* (which means a monthly bank charge), *deposit amount*, and running total. The figure $1,130.96 is the beginning balance in this example. The deposits have been added and payments or deductions have been subtracted.

SIMPLIFIED SUCCESS

CHECK NUMBER	DATE	DESCRIPTION	PAYMENT AMOUNT	✓	FEE	DEPOSIT	$ 1130.96
201	7/14	Life Insurance Co. Monthly payment	$ 52 41	✓	$	$	52.41 / 1078.55
	7/15	Electric Co. Monthly Bill	62 00	✓			62.00 / 1016.55
	7/15	Super Market Groceries	71 45	✓			71.45 / 945.10
	7/17	Phone / Internet Monthly bill	119 07	✓			119.07 / 826.03
	7/18	Convenience Store Snacks	5 97	✓			5.97 / 820.06
202	7/18	Mortgage Co. House payment	717 56	✓			717.56 / 102.50
	7/19	Deposit Paycheck		✓		1,549 27	1,549.27 / 1,651.77
	7/19	Savings	100 —	✓			100.00 / 1,551.77
	7/20	Doughnuts	8 43	✓			8.43 / 1,543.34
	7/20	Bowling Alley Game & shoes	10 72	✓			10.72 / 1,532.62
	7/21	Gift Shop Wedding gift	31 41	✓			31.41 / 1,501.21
	7/22	Workout Facility Monthly bill	25 00	✓			25.00 / 1,476.21
203	7/24	Donation Hurricane Relief	50 —				50.00 / 1,426.21
	7/25	Magazine Subscription	14 98				14.98 / 1,411.23
	7/26	Credit Card Payment in full	276 59	✓			276.59 / 1,134.64
	7/27	Super Market water & napkins	7 50	✓			7.50 / 1,127.14
	7/27	Jewelry store Ring repair	35 00				35.00 / 1,092.14
	7/28	Deposit Birthday gift		✓		50 00	50.00 / 1,142.14
	7/29	Water Company monthly bill	42 54				42.54 / 1,099.60
	7/30	ATM withdraw Cash	60 —	✓			60.— / 1,039.60

CHAPTER TWO: PART I

Check writing is becoming a thing of the past as most transactions are done electronically in this world of high tech. Debit cards are usually associated with checking accounts where purchases must be tracked with receipts. It is important to enter all transactions into your register at the end of every day for you to keep an accurate balance. This will help you avoid the unnecessary fees associated with the overdrawn account discussed earlier. This is a responsibility or area where you must be consistent, and if so, you will be rewarded with a feeling of accomplishment and the absence of unnecessary fees.

Compounding Interest from the Borrowing Side

Compounding interest is commonly referred to as "The Eighth Wonder of the World" by people who know how powerful this concept is. Don't ask me what the other seven are, but if they are as great as compounding interest then they are grand!

When I first began my banking career, I didn't know much about money, other than I liked making and saving it. As I worked with money every day, I began to understand how money could work *for* me and how it could work *against* me. It all depended on what side of the equation I was on, the borrowing side or the saving side. Let's look at the borrowing side first.

The borrowing side *costs* money. This is how we bankers make our living. Bankers make loans and charge interest and fees on the amount of money loaned. Borrowers, in turn, make payments which include a monthly portion of the amount borrowed PLUS interest. Interest is a large portion of many financial institution's income. The amount of interest you will pay during your lifetime is ultimately your decision. Most of us will need to borrow money at some point during our lifetime, so let's learn to borrow smart.

Managing Credit Cards

We all love our credit cards. These little pieces of plastic fit into our wallets or purses just perfectly, and they feel so good in our hands. Most of us have one or two and some people have eight to ten! The credit card is not necessarily a must have in today's world, but it is a nice compliment to the debit card. A credit card carries a pre-authorized borrowing limit, which means the person who owns the card has a pre-set limit he or she can spend. That limit is usually $5,000 or $10,000 but can be as little as $500, or as much as $100,000, depending on the person's financial capabilities.

When you use your card to purchase an item, the cost of that item is added to your credit card balance. This balance is an accumulation of purchases you have made with your card over a 30-day period. Once that 30-day period is over, you receive a statement from the credit card company, listing the purchases you made and the amount of each. It also shows the total amount you owe the credit card company. At this point, you have two options:

1) Pay the small monthly payment by the due date or,
2) Pay the entire balance in full by the due date.

CHAPTER TWO: PART I

You like the option of holding on to your money, so you elect option #1. Let's review this option. You go online and make your credit card payment or send it by mail only to leave the remaining balance on the card. The bill is paid and out of your mind for another month. This sounds harmless, however, it can be devastating to your finances. The subtlety you forget about is that this card is issued by a company that needs to make money to stay in business. The way this company makes its money is by charging interest on the remaining balance.

Let's assume you made $400.00 in purchases during a 30-day period. Your statement comes in and your payment is due in 30 days. The minimum payment is $25.00, and you pay only the $25.00. You assume your balance is now $375.00, but that is incorrect, and this is where it hurts. The balance is $385.00. You paid $25.00 but only reduced your balance by $15.00.

"How can that be?" you ask. The interest rates on most credit cards range from 14-28% meaning $10.00 went to pay the interest. What happens in the next 30 days? You purchase more items with your card and your bill is now $700.00. You pay the $25.00 again and your balance only decreases $9.00. This time, $16.00 went to pay the interest.

"Why," you ask? Because your balance is larger. The larger the balance on your card, the more interest you pay, thus reducing the amount you are paying toward the balance. Again, this is how credit card companies make money.

So how do you avoid this? <u>*Pay the balance of your card in full every month without exception.*</u> Only charge as much as you can afford to pay in full when the bill arrives! Paying your balance in full *every* month is the *only* way to use a credit card.

Credit card companies are some of the biggest and most lucrative companies in the world. They make billions and billions of dollars a year off people who do not pay their balances in full every month. Please avoid this financial issue. If you are in over your head as you read this, please cut up your card, call the company, close the account and begin paying as much as you can toward the balance every month.

Paying off your credit card bill every month is a fundamental principle you should commit to. By doing this, you are avoiding interest that comes with maintaining a balance.

This one decision will save you thousands of dollars over your lifetime and help set you on the path to financial freedom.

Financing an Automobile

Let's talk about one of our favorite items, the automobile. We all love a new vehicle. We love to test drive them; we love the smell of the interior; we love the way it looks, so shiny and brand-new sitting on the car lot. We are captivated by all the amenities that come with the newer models. Now let's talk about how this could apply to you:

You've seen the TV ads and you've been thinking about the clunker you've been driving, and the repair bills you've had to endure. Then, it hits you; it's time to take a drive down to the car dealership! You stroll around the lot gazing at those beauties and finally, you see one you love! After a few minutes, a salesperson comes out to welcome you to his dealership. He asks if you have found one you like, and if you'd like to take it

CHAPTER TWO: PART I

for a test drive. He hands you the keys and off you go. Wow, this is the life! You slide into that leather seat, the new car smell is wonderful, and then your eye catches all the gadgets and buttons on the control panel. You are captivated by the experience as you ride off in the new car trying to process everything that's happened in the last 20 minutes. Once you get back to the dealership, you have a feel for the new vehicle, you are familiar with it and like the way it handles.

Now, you are faced with a decision; do you pursue the purchase or not? You should decide on the answer to this question before you get back to the dealership. If this is the vehicle you want, then hopefully you've done your research on this make and model (whether new or used) beforehand and are ready to negotiate the steps of this purchase. If you haven't done your research, my suggestion is to not rush into it.

A salesperson makes money when you purchase a vehicle. He may receive a salary but works mainly on commission, meaning he gets a certain dollar amount every time he sells a vehicle. He will be prepared to do his job so you should be prepared to do yours.

It is my opinion you should buy a used vehicle for these reasons:

- A new vehicle is higher priced, which means you will have a larger loan to repay.
- A large loan means you will pay back a large amount of interest and fees.
- A new vehicle loses, on average, nearly 10% of its value as soon as you drive it off the lot and 34% of its value in the first 3 years.

SIMPLIFIED SUCCESS

- A used vehicle has a smaller purchase price (which gives you a smaller loan), thereby giving you more freedom to reduce your debt quickly.

From my financial point of view, buying a high priced, new vehicle is not worth the "new" experience especially if you must finance a large portion of it.

If you must borrow for a vehicle, buy an inexpensive one, make a down payment and pay it off as quickly as you can. A vehicle purchased and driven for personal use will seldom make you any money. The more you pay for a vehicle means the more you must borrow, which means more of everything you don't need: higher payments, higher insurance, and higher taxes.

Sure, a vehicle is a necessity and always will be; however, a decent one is all you need. A vehicle that costs $10,000 will get you to work just as well as one that costs $50,000.

Let's look at an example of two vehicle purchases and what they will cost their new owners:

	Buyer #1	Buyer #2
Purchase price	$10,000	$50,000
Sales Tax 6%	600	3,000
Warranty	700	1,800
Total Financed	$11,300	$54,800
Interest Cost at 4.9%	868	10,048
Total Cost of Vehicle	$12,168	$64,848
Loan Term	36 months	84 months
Monthly Payment Amount	**$338**	**$772**

CHAPTER TWO: PART I

The total cost for Buyer #1 is $12,168, which includes $868 in interest costs over the three-year period. The total cost for Buyer #2 is $64,848 which includes over $10,000 in interest over the seven-year period. Buyer #2 bought an expensive vehicle and borrowed so much money that his total payout is almost $53,000 more than Buyer #1.

If you add insurance, a down payment, annual tax, and other possible charges, you can see how an expensive vehicle can drain your cash flow and take as many as seven years to pay off.

You may say, "If I buy a used vehicle, I will have more repairs." Yes, that could be the case, but chances are they will be few and far between. Buyer #1 bought a used vehicle and has a payment that is $434 less than Buyer #2. Assuming no repairs for the first year, he/she will be able to save $5,208 in the first year alone!

To sum it up, the less expensive vehicle has a payment that is much lower and will be paid off four years sooner, allowing you to save money towards something else you want, like a house!

Buying Your First Home

Most people desire a home of their own. Some people rent and some people buy. Renting is not a bad option and should not be deemed as "throwing money away" as some people say. When people rent, they are purchasing 30 days of shelter for a specified monthly rent amount.

People rent for all sorts of reasons; they are young and

can't afford a down payment, they may not be staying in one place very long because of their job situation, or they may choose to rent because they don't want to be bothered with the maintenance and repairs that come with owning their own home. Whatever the reason, more and more people are renting. As of 2019, the home ownership rate was lower than it was in 1978.

If you choose to rent, don't go out and find the best place that money can buy. Look for something reasonably priced. It won't be your dream home, but at this point you're not looking for your dream home. You're not going to stay there forever, so find a decent, clean place where you can live for a certain amount of time and one that is within your price range. This will allow you to have extra money at the end of each month, which you can save for a down payment on a house.

The same is true when looking for your first home. Beware of buying the biggest and most expensive house you can afford. You shouldn't stretch yourself to the max based on your income. Furthermore, you definitely want to avoid maxing out the loan payment based on two incomes. Your banker will tell you the maximum price you can afford based on your total household income and debt payments. He/she will give you information which will include payments based on a 30-year loan. Why 30 years? Because financing on 30 years keeps your payment amount lower. Mortgage loans are generally quoted on 15 and 30-year terms. Most people don't opt for the 15-year mortgage because the shorter term causes their monthly payment to be higher. Your banker wants to help you achieve your dream of home ownership, so he/she will make it as easy

CHAPTER TWO: PART I

as possible and will work hard to get you qualified.

Your human nature will try to take over at this point. The banker told you the maximum amount you can borrow and off you go to find the most expensive house you can afford, not thinking about how much this decision will cost you in the long run.

In the next few paragraphs, I will give you a strategy that includes borrowing less money and paying it back quickly. Your #1 goal using this strategy is to find a house that is well within your means, a nice house that is less expensive, and finance it over a 15-year period. I have often told my daughter and my nephew, "I have spoken with many people who want to buy a big house with a small down payment. I want you to buy a smaller house with a big down payment." The following scenarios will show you how money and time can make a huge difference in your financial future.

Let's look at these two examples:

Couple # 1 – Kaitlyn and Jordan go to their local bank and talk with their loan officer. They have saved $18,000 for a down payment and closing costs and are looking forward to their visit. Their combined annual salaries total $80,000. Their banker runs some preliminary calculations and finds that with both incomes, the maximum amount they can afford to spend is $260,000.

Off they go to look for their dream home. They find a new home - two stories with a full basement, four bedrooms and three baths. The asking price on the home is $269,000, and they agree to purchase the house for $260,000 after negotiations. Kaitlyn and Jordan have found their dream home and they are happy.

They make their way back to the bank to inform their loan officer that they have a contract on a home. The banker then gives them some options. She informs them that they have the required minimum of 5% for the down payment, which is $13,000 (.05 x $260,000 = $13,000). They are financing 95% or $247,000 of the purchase price, and their mortgage rate will be 4.50%. Their payment is $1,252 per month on a 30-year loan.

Because the banker is trying to help them get the house they want, she quotes payments based on a 30-year payout, which means Kaitlyn and Jordan will have a lower payment. While stretching out the years calculates into a lower payment, it also means they will pay much more interest over the life of the loan.

The $1,252 monthly payment is only the beginning. There are costs associated with the loan. These are called closing costs and are based on the amount borrowed. The more money borrowed, the higher the total. These costs and fees are generally 2-3% of the borrowed amount or a minimum of $4,940 in this case (.02 x $247,000 = $4,940). I won't go into detail about these expenses, but I will list them here, so you'll have an idea of what is required when you begin the search for your house. Some of these one-time fees consist of: Title Search/Title Insurance, Appraisal, Origination and Recording. Other costs, including Homeowner's Insurance and Property Tax will most likely be escrowed. Private Mortgage Insurance is another charge that could be added to the monthly payment. These monthly expenses are explained in more detail below.

Escrow - Property Tax and Homeowner Insurance:

CHAPTER TWO: PART I

Escrow is a monthly amount paid by the borrower to satisfy the future payment of property taxes and property insurance on the home. This monthly amount is added in with the loan payment. Property taxes are based on the value of the home and are calculated by percentage. The higher the price paid for the home, the higher the tax bill will be. The tax rate for the county in which I live is $10.50 for every $1,000 of property value. (Property tax rates in Kentucky are some of the lowest in the nation). If you live in a state that has high property tax rates, the amount of escrow would be higher. Please remember this when shopping for a home. In this case, the tax rate on a $260,000 home would be $2,730 annually for the county property tax. If the house is in the city, another $700 annually must be added for city property tax. For this example, let's say the house is outside the city limits making the tax bill $2,730.

The next expense is property insurance, commonly referred to as homeowner's insurance. For this example, the price of the annual policy is $1,200 per year. The bank adds the annual cost of the property tax and homeowner's insurance together, which totals $3,930. This amount is divided by 12 (number of months in a year), and the amount of $328 (the escrowed amount) is added to the $1,252 payment, making the total payment $1,580.

Private Mortgage Insurance (PMI): PMI is an insurance that protects the bank from losing money in case it must foreclose on the house. If the loan is above 80% of the appraised amount, PMI is generally required. The monthly cost of this insurance varies depending on the size of the loan. The more money borrowed, the more PMI costs. (Because of the detailed characteristics of PMI, I won't use this fee in the payment calculations.)

Now, let's break down the $1,580 initial monthly payment and see how Kaitlyn and Jordan fare:

Principal – Amount going toward the reduction of their loan	$326
Interest – Borrowed amount $247,000 x 4.50% interest rate	$926
Property Tax - One month of escrow	$228
Homeowner's Insurance – One month of escrow	$100
Total Monthly Payment	**$1,580**

Notice how much interest is being paid to the bank and how little is being paid on the principal balance of the loan. Now, don't get upset with the bank. These dollar amounts are a direct result of two items: 1) the amount of money borrowed, and 2) the interest rate on the loan. Kaitlyn and Jordan decided to borrow the maximum amount and the interest rates are determined by the overall market.

The banker did her job by giving Kaitlyn and Jordan their options, but it was Kaitlyn and Jordan who ultimately decided how much money they borrowed.

Assuming insurance and property tax remain the same over the life of the loan (both will increase), $1,580 is the monthly payment amount Kaitlyn and Jordan are stuck with for 30 years. A quick calculation shows by multiplying $1,580 x 360 (the number of months in 30 years) they are going to pay $568,800 over a thirty-year period to live in their $260,000 dream home. This is a heavy price to pay for shelter in the high life! This is one harsh example of how money and time can work against you.

Now let's review the scenario of the couple who buys a

CHAPTER TWO: PART I

less expensive house.

Couple #2 – Bradley and Lauren visit their hometown bank. They have $18,000 for a down payment and closing costs and the same income of the previous couple, which is $80,000. Their financial situation also allows them to qualify for a $260,000 loan, but they elect to go with a nice, but smaller house that is 15 years old and has three bedrooms and two baths. The asking price for this home is $159,000 and they settle on a purchase price of $150,000.

They make their way back to the bank and the banker lays out their options. They will be borrowing 90% of the value of the home or $135,000 and financing the home for 15 years at a lower rate of 4.00% (rates are lower on 15-year mortgages). Based on these numbers, their payment is $999 per month. Their closing costs are 2% of the amount borrowed ($135,000) which equals $2,700. You arrive at this cost by multiplying .02 x $135,000.

Property taxes are $1,575 and homeowner's insurance will be $825, making the total of these two figures $2,400, which will be escrowed. Just like in the example with Couple #1, this number is divided by 12, which adds $200 to the $999 for a total payment of $1,199.

Now, let's break down the $1,199 initial monthly payment and see how Bradley and Lauren fare:

Principal – Amount going toward the reduction of their loan	$549
Interest – Borrowed amount $135,000 at 4.00% interest rate	$450
Property Tax – One month of escrow	$131
Homeowner's Insurance – One month of escrow	$ 69
Total Monthly Payment	**$1,199**

47

SIMPLIFIED SUCCESS

Now, compare the figures of each couple. By starting with a smaller loan, Bradley and Lauren are way ahead of Couple #1. By going with the 15-year loan instead of the 30-year loan, they have already eliminated 15 years of payments. The 15-year loan allowed them to begin reducing the principal balance much faster. Let's take it one step further and review the results over the 15-year period. Multiplying the $1,199 payment by 180 (the number of months in 15 years) the amount comes to $215,820.

Not only will Bradley and Lauren pay off their house in half the time, they will spend nearly $353,000 less than Couple #1.

After 15 years, Bradley and Lauren's house will be paid off and they can look forward to some great options. On the other hand, Kaitlyn and Jordan will still owe $163,000 on their "dream home" and will continue to be saddled with a large house payment for another 15 years! If you add in the additional money Kaitlyn and Jordan will have to spend on utility costs to live in their dream home, you can see why a more expensive house can be a poor decision for a young couple just getting started.

A house is very costly! Yes, the value of it should increase over time and yes, you must have a place to live, but buying a more expensive house than needed is not a good way to start out.

Here are some other important things to think about: Couple #2 has a monthly payment which is $381 less than Couple #1. While Couple #1 has enough to make their payment

CHAPTER TWO: PART I

and enough to take care of the necessities, they don't have much left over for other fun activities. Couple #2, however, elected to buy a less expensive house, which gives them extra cash at the end of each month. They now have the freedom to enjoy an occasional dinner out and other hobbies or activities.

They saw the benefit of living within their means and made a wise decision to purchase a smaller house and borrow less.

Couple #2 could also take this money and invest it. For example, if they invested the $381 each month earning 7.00%, their savings would grow to $121,678 at the end of the same 15-year period. I will go into more detail about this a little later in the chapter.

Just a few pages back you read about Couple #1's mistake of borrowing too much money. You also read about the excellent debt reduction strategy of Couple #2. Now, there is one more strategy I want to mention here. The theme is the same, live within your means, but this savings strategy is a little different from the Couple #2 scenario described earlier.

Couple #3 – Corey and Annie are looking to purchase a home and have decided on one that won't strain their budget, just like Couple #2. They buy the house for $150,000 and they borrow $135,000 just like Couple #2. But, instead of financing for 15 years with a total payment of $1,199, they finance it for 30 years. As they've learned, a 30-year term lowers their payment.

Let's review the breakdown of their initial payment of $884 based on a 30-year loan:

SIMPLIFIED SUCCESS

Principal – Amount going toward the reduction of their loan	$178
Interest – Borrowed amount $135,000 at 4.50% interest rate	$506
Property Tax – One month of escrow	$131
Homeowner's Insurance – One month of escrow	$ 69
Total Monthly Payment	**$884**

As expected, the total payment is less because of the 30-year term. So, just to refresh; Couple #2 has a payment of $1,199 and Couple #3 has a payment of $884. The difference in the two is $315, which comes mainly from the principal amount. By paying less principal Couple #3 is not reducing their loan as quickly as Couple #2. So, if they're not reducing their loan as quickly then they must use the $315 savings to make up for the extra interest they will be paying over the life of their 30-year loan.

In the example shown, Couple #3 is paying 4.50% on the money borrowed. Their $315 savings will need to be invested in an account that will earn more than 4.50% for this strategy to work. Furthermore, the entire $315 will need to be invested every month for the next 30 years at a rate greater than their 4.50% loan rate for this strategy to work well.

For example, if their $315 monthly investment earns an average of 7.00% annually, they will do very well. If they only average 3.00% annually, they will not.

Now, let's get back to you:

It comes down to these factors you must commit to if you plan to use this strategy; 1) You must have the discipline to invest the difference every month, resisting the temptation to spend it; 2) You must find an investment which has an extended track record that will exceed your loan rate over a 15-30-year

CHAPTER TWO: PART I

period, and 3) You must stay the course. If you can commit to this strategy, and your average annual savings interest rate is higher than your loan rate, you can accumulate enough savings to off-set the interest paid over the 30-year period.

Both strategies require you to stay focused, disciplined, and consistent. The 15-year option used by Couple #2 is a conservative approach versus the 30-year calculated risk approach used by Couple #3. Both are tremendous strategies for reducing your interest cost over time and one of these approaches should suit your investing style.

A personal testimony:

Christy and I bought our first house in 1987 and paid $47,500 for it. It was a 1200 square foot brick home with a two-car garage on a nice corner lot in a middle-class neighborhood. It wasn't fancy, but it served us well. Both of us worked and we literally lived on one income and saved the other. I was making $17,000 a year in the banking business and Christy was making $15,000 as a first-grade teacher.

We were married in 1985 and were able to save $18,000 during this two-year period. We used $15,000 as a down payment, borrowing $32,500 at 11.5% interest! I know this sky-high rate is unheard of now, but interest was extremely high in the early 80's and had actually come down to 11.5% in 1987.

We initially financed our house over a 15-year period, just like Couple #2, but realized we could afford to pay more than the $380 monthly payment. At first, we began paying $20 extra per month and before we knew it, we began paying $500, then $600 per month. Instead of placing this extra money into a lower rate savings account, we decided to pay it on the principal balance of our home loan. We made our last payment on this house four years and eleven months after we bought it.

By purchasing a smaller, less expensive home with a large down payment, we were able to pay off our home much more quickly and avoid much of the interest expense that goes along with borrowing money for a home.

From this one financial exercise, we were able to reduce our interest cost drastically. After we sold our first home, we applied the proceeds of the sale to our next home purchase and continued with the same debt reduction strategy. We realized that borrowing money for personal items, even a house, was money working against us.

My advice for you is to study the strategies of Couples #2 and #3 and decide which is best for you. Each can work well with planning, discipline, and consistency. Just remember the number one rule: <u>*Buy a house within your means!*</u>

The larger the purchase price, the larger the loan, the larger the payment, the smaller your bank account! On the other hand, the smaller the purchase price, the smaller the loan, the smaller the payment, which means you have more money to invest giving it a chance to work *for* you!

CHAPTER TWO:

Financial Health — Making Money Work for You
Part II

Compounding Interest from the Saving Side

As I mentioned before, compounding interest is an amazing concept. It is truly a phenomenon, and if you begin saving early and systematically your accounts can grow to more than you could ever imagine.

Money is a powerful tool. If it is abused or not used correctly, it can possibly ruin your life and your financial dreams. On the other hand, being careful with money and using it correctly can enhance your life and in time, allow you to enhance the lives of those around you.

Compounding works best and money works hardest for you when you begin saving early. Time is the essential ingredient when it comes to compounding interest. The concept is this: *the interest you make begins to earn interest.* The more interest you earn now, the more interest you will earn in the future. Not only are you investing your own money which earns interest, but your interest also earns interest! The longer time-period you have for this process to work, the better.

Let me use a snowball analogy. Think of the process of building a snowman. Snowmen can only be made when the snow sticks. You begin with a snowball and then gently roll it around until more snow begins to accumulate. The process is a little slower at first as you try to get a snowball big enough to roll around. Once you get to the point where you have a decent sized snowball, it begins to grow rather quickly. Before you know it, you have a ball of snow you can barely push! Now, let's take it one step further. What if you were able to push that snowball around for 24 hours non-stop? It would be as big as a mountain! The process began with a little snowball and it grew as it gathered more snow….and that snow gathered more snow. The continuous pushing and the time factor allowed it to grow to an enormous size! This is how compounding interest works. As you begin saving money, a smaller sum takes a little more time to grow, but as you continue to save it begins to pile up! The more time you have, the more money you can accumulate. This is how money works for you!

Compounding Interest Chart

To the right is a chart of two individuals who are the same age and began working at the same company, at the same time with the same salary:

One who saved for the first ten years and one who waited.

Saving Now versus Later
($200 per month compounded daily at 7.00%)

	The Early Bird		The Procrastinator	
Year	Contribution	Savings	Contribution	Savings
1	$2,400	$2,493	$ 0	$ 0
2	2,400	5,166	0	0
3	2,400	8,032	0	0
4	2,400	11,106	0	0
5	2,400	14,402	0	0
6	2,400	17,936	0	0
7	2,400	21,725	0	0
8	2,400	25,789	0	0
9	2,400	30,147	0	0
10	2,400	34,819	0	0
11	0	37,336	$2,400	$2,493
12	0	40,035	2,400	5,166
13	0	42,929	2,400	8,032
14	0	46,033	2,400	11,106
15	0	49,360	2,400	14,402
16	0	52,928	2,400	17,936
17	0	56,755	2,400	21,725
18	0	60,858	2,400	25,789
19	0	65,257	2,400	30,147
20	0	69.974	2,400	34,819
21	0	75,033	2,400	39,829
22	0	80,457	2,400	45,201
23	0	86,273	2,400	50,962
24	0	92,510	2,400	57,138
25	0	99,197	2,400	63,763
26	0	106,368	2,400	70,864
27	0	114,057	2,400	78,480
28	0	122,303	2,400	86,647
29	0	131,144	2,400	95,403
30	0	140,625	2,400	104,793
31	0	150,791	2,400	114,862
32	0	161,691	2,400	125,658
33	0	173,380	2,400	137,235
34	0	185,914	2,400	149,648
35	0	199,353	2,400	162,959
36	0	213,765	2,400	177,233
37	0	229,218	2,400	192,538
38	0	245,788	2,400	208,949
39	0	263,556	2,400	226,547
40	0	282,608	2,400	245,417

SIMPLIFIED SUCCESS

This is amazing! No wonder compounding interest is called "The Eighth Wonder of the World." The Early Bird invested a total of $24,000 and stopped after year ten. *The Procrastinator started at year 11 and invested for the next 30 years but still had less!* Early Bird was able to accumulate $282,608, while Procrastinator invested a much greater sum of $72,000 but only saved $245,417.

To sum it up, Early Bird invested $48,000 less and saved $37,191 more, an $85,191 difference! If Early Bird didn't stop, but continued to invest for the full 40 years, the results for her would be an investment of $96,000 with total savings of $528,025! Can you imagine investing the sum of $96,000 and coming away with $528,000! That's incredible! You can see how it pays to start early.

This is a great visual of how compounding works. The one who began saving early gave her money time to grow. By investing early, her money began earning interest and over time, her snowball grew larger and larger. This is a great comparison and one that shows you firsthand how important it is to begin saving early and consistently.

I wanted to show the illustration using the smaller amount of $200 per month, because this amount is more attainable for those just starting out. As you settle into your career, begin investing in a retirement account and increase your savings rate as your salary grows. In other words, increase your investment percentage every time you get a raise.

Important: Please don't stop investing after year ten! This illustration demonstrates how important it is to save early,

CHAPTER TWO: PART II

not save early and stop. This chart shows the amazing impact of compounding interest. To create this illustration I used the website www.thecalculatorsite.com and verified the numbers at www.financialmentor.com.

Saving for Retirement

Now let's talk about how you can use this saving principle in your everyday life. You may work for a company or possibly will someday. Many companies have 401k savings plans they offer their employees. The 401k is a retirement account which gives you the opportunity to automatically invest a portion of your paycheck. This is called "paying yourself first." Generally, the company you work for will match a certain portion of your investment. This range is usually 3% - 6% of your salary.

Let's say your company offers a 3% match. This means if you have 3% of your paycheck automatically deposited into your 401k account, your employer will match it. This is free money! This is what we call a "100% return on your investment!" Some employers offer a 6% match, and that's even better. Your employer may offer a 50% match, meaning you would need to have 6% of your paycheck deposited to your 401k account before your employer would contribute 3%. Take advantage of either of these scenarios as soon as you are eligible to participate. It's free money, and it's going into your account!

Always maximize this benefit as it will add up in a big way over time. Two especially important sidebars here: *Whatever percentage amount you decide to invest, have it automatically deducted from your paycheck to avoid the temptation of spending the money. Secondly, you are investing "pretax" dollars, which means your contributions are taken from your paycheck before taxes are deducted. This allows you to pay less income tax while also reducing your city, county, and school taxes in the process.*

Another product named the Roth Individual Retirement Account (Roth IRA) is an account that is too good for anyone to pass up, especially a younger person. <u>*A Roth IRA is an account that offers tax-free growth and tax-free withdraws in retirement.*</u> These accounts are funded with after-tax dollars. This doesn't help you lower your income tax initially, but the earnings are tax free once you reach the age of 59 ½. Roth IRA's can be opened at most banks and similar financial institutions on location or online. Please take a close look at a Roth IRA as it could be one of the best investments you will ever make.

Now that you have your money and your *free* money from your employer being deposited into your retirement account each month, you can begin to watch it grow. Your account will likely have multiple options as to how you can invest your money. These investments generally consist of stocks, bonds, real estate, and fixed income funds, among others. You have the authority to direct your money into any of these investments you wish, however, these investment categories are not created equal. Some investments may give you a higher return than others, but also expose your money to more risk. While you can make money quickly with stock investments, you can also lose it quickly in a downturn of the

CHAPTER TWO: PART II
───────────

stock market. However, over long periods of time, stock investing has proven to be the investment of choice because of the stock market's proven track record.

There are numerous financial websites that can give you the direction you need as you invest over your lifetime. There are also financial planners who are particularly good at laying out the fundamentals for you as you begin your journey of investing. Please remember, the main point is to start saving. The earlier you begin, the better off you will be financially.

Budgeting

Speaking of financial freedom brings the good ol' budget to mind. Some people hate to hear the word "budget" because it conjures up mental images of boundaries, limits, restrictions, or worse, handcuffs! People tend to think of a budget as the exact opposite of financial freedom.

I understand the thought process people go through when they hear the words, "you need to budget." But I also understand if you don't have some financial limits in your life or marriage, you will never be able to achieve financial freedom. A budget *is* a set of boundaries, limits and restrictions. Understanding why they are there and what they do, will give you a better appreciation of what a budget can do for your finances.

Here is an analogy. Let's say you have a toddler and exploring around the house is one of her favorite activities. Everything she sees she wants to put in her mouth. She finds a marble on the floor, she grabs the hairbrush, she chews on the

SIMPLIFIED SUCCESS

dog's toy, or she finds the pacifier that has been under the desk for three days. In her eyes, this is good for her. In your eyes, this is not good for many reasons. You, as her parent, know that she needs boundaries, limits and restrictions to keep her healthy. It's the same when it comes to money.

It's a good financial practice to have boundaries in place so you can afford to pay bills and plan for a great financial future for you and your family. Let me give you a little of my background so you can see how I came to learn to budget. I enjoyed saving money as a kid. I enjoyed polishing my dad's shoes and making 25 cents per pair. I would polish four pairs of his dress shoes, and he would pay me $1.00. My brother Rich and I would mow the grass with a push mower. I would mow the front for $2.00, and he would mow the back for $2.00. When I received money from relatives for Christmas, it most always went into my savings account. Like many of you, if I wanted something, I had to save to buy it. I remember seeing a baby blue Schwinn 10-speed bicycle I wanted. The cost was $150 back in 1974. I kept saving my allowance and my work money and bought it when I had enough.

No, I didn't have a budget at that age and didn't even know what a budget was, but I knew I wanted that bike, and I also knew the money I spent on other things was taking away money that was earmarked for my bike. I might have bought an occasional pack of football or baseball cards for a dime, but I didn't spend dollars on anything! Before I knew it, I had enough to buy the bike and was so proud I had purchased it with my own money. This way of thinking followed me all the way into my marriage.

CHAPTER TWO: PART II

After Christy and I married, we decided I would be the Chief Financial Officer of the Ledford household, which had two employees, Christy and me. The only real qualification I had was that I worked at the bank and the fact that she really didn't want to handle the finances. So, it was settled and I became the CFO. Obviously, the banking business kept my mind on money and how it worked. I had a desire to make the most of our finances and to not waste our money on things we didn't need. Once we settled into our apartment and Christy gained employment as a first-grade teacher, we began to review our current financial situation and plan for our financial future. I began reading personal finance books on how to manage money and everything I read included a chapter on budgeting. The more I read, the more I realized there had to be something beneficial about having a budget.

One day, Christy and I sat down and discussed this and decided we would give it a try. I found a basic budget worksheet in one of the books and began by using our net income (bring home pay). I proceeded to go down each category and put in amounts where I knew the exact cost. Examples of our fixed cost expenses were rent, water, electric, insurance, phone, car payment, and so on. Next came other items that were not fixed but variable, meaning they vary from month to month. Those were food, clothing, eating out, entertainment, gas for the car, etc.

On the next page is a budget worksheet nearly identical to the one I used over 30 years ago as we began to gain control of our finances. As I stated earlier, there are many versions, so you should be able to find one that suits your financial situation.

Monthly Household Net Income Budget Worksheet

In Section I, you will enter your net monthly income and all other income you plan to receive. In Section II, you will enter your monthly expenses. By using net income, payroll deductions have already been deducted.

Section I: Net Monthly Income

	Estimated	Actual
1st Person: List net monthly income from all jobs		
2nd Person: List net monthly income from all jobs		
Bonus Income		
Reimbursements		
Cash/Gift Cards		
Child Support		
Interest Received		
Other: List additional income		
Totals		

Section II: Monthly Expenses

	Estimated	Actual
Rent/Mortgage/Taxes & Insurance		
Home Equity Loan Payment/Other Payment		
Car - #1 Payment		
Car - #2 Payment		
Car - Insurance		
Car – Gasoline		
Car – Maintenance/Repair		
Car – Parking/Commuting Costs		
Electric Bill		
Water Bill		
Gas/Heating Bill		
Phone Bills (Mobile, Land line)		
TV (Cable, Satellite) Bill		
Internet Access Bill		
Garbage Bill		
Groceries		
Dining Out		
Clothing		
Lawn Care		
Household Repairs		
Credit Card Payment (full balance recommended/or payment)		
Daycare/Babysitting		
Pet Care		
Medical/Dental		
Gym Membership		
Church/Charitable Giving		
Recreation		
Vacation		
Spending Money/Miscellaneous		
Gift Giving		
Savings		
Totals		

Section III: RESULTS

	Estimated	Actual
TOTAL NET MONTHLY INCOME		
TOTAL MONTHLY EXPENSES		
THE DIFFERENCE (subtract total expenses from total income)		

(This shows how much you are over/under your budget)

CHAPTER TWO: PART II

This is a simple household budget worksheet. To find one, just do an internet search for "monthly household budget," and you will come up with millions of hits. Click on a few and find one that fits your style. This can also be written by hand or you can find one in Excel format.

The next part takes a little more time. First, you will need to list your income. The budget worksheet you are using will determine whether you use your "gross income" or your "net income." "Gross" is your total before taxes and any other payroll deductions. "Net" is your total after taxes and any other payroll deductions. It doesn't make any difference which one you use, but make sure you use a worksheet designed for one or the other. Personally, I like the "net income" worksheet because net income is the true amount I have to work with.

General household budgets are guidelines as to how much you should be spending in all categories. Once you have decided on the budget worksheet you are going to use and have listed your monthly income, you can begin figuring how much you spent over the last 12 months. The best way to do this is to review your bank statements and log every expense you had for the 12-month period by placing each expense into one of the categories listed on your budget worksheet. You will also need to review your end-of-year credit card summary for expenses and log those the same way.

Let me give you an example: You review each of your 12 monthly bank statements and credit card statements and find you spent a total of $1,800 on dining out. Since you are budgeting for a 12-month period you divide $1,800 by 12, which equals $150 per month. This is the amount you averaged spending dining out each month. This is your monthly budget figure for the "Dining Out" category unless you decide to lower or raise it. You are to do this for each category listed on your budget worksheet. The fixed expenses are easiest because these amounts are the same month after month (rent, car payment, etc.). Your variable expenses will take a little more time. Some other places to check for expenditures are cash receipts and receipts from pre-paid "loaded" cards. Other income sources may include tax refunds, birthday gifts, gift cards, yard sales, side jobs, etc.

Your goal through this process is to identify your total income and your total expenses and list each in the appropriate budget category. Once these monthly numbers are inserted under the "Estimated" column, you are ready to begin tracking future expenses. Important note: Your monthly "Estimated" budgeted expense total must equal the amount of your total monthly income. The "Savings" line item will be the area you can adjust to help balance the two.

Now you are ready to begin tracking your future income and expenses. *Your goal is to track every bit of income that you receive and every expense that goes out.* This seemed impossible to me until Christy and I agreed to try it.

Once we understood the benefit of having a budget, we decided to track every penny for six months. Just the thought of this seemed like a crazy idea. Tracking every penny? Aren't we going a little overboard? Well, it was a commitment to a financial exercise and, we believed, a commitment to excellence. Do it right or don't do it at all was our thinking. At first, it was hard because I would forget about the candy bar I

CHAPTER TWO: PART II

purchased with cash or the $5.00 car wash where I didn't get a receipt. But at the end of each day, we would recount what we had spent and come up with some missed expenses and add them to our sheet. At the end of each week, I would tally the cash purchases, checks and other expenses and keep a running total for each category. This weekly checkup enabled us to see if we were on track for the month. This was beneficial for us in three ways: 1) It was making us aware of how we were spending our money, 2) it was giving us an accurate picture of our finances, and 3) it made us acutely aware of our financial boundaries the budget had created.

Once we tracked and listed our expenses for the month on a separate sheet of paper, I would add the expenses and list each total in its appropriate category. We could then see how we spent our money and how we compared to the budget figure for each category. Each line item budget figure was our guideline. If we went over the budget figure in one area, we had to spend less in others to make up the difference. We adjusted several categories over the first few months, increasing some line items and lowering others to fit our lifestyle. One thing that Christy and I loved to do was to go out and eat on Friday nights. Both of us worked, and it was just a pleasure to relax with each other and enjoy a nice meal. Instead of cutting back in this area, we decided to lower one of the other budget figures. We enjoyed eating out, and it was reasonable (usually Golden Corral), so we went out every Friday.

We diligently tracked almost every penny for six months, which set our financial course for the rest of our lives. The one thing we realized during that six-month period is that we weren't wasting much money. Sure, there were some small items we bought that we could have done without, but there weren't many. Tracking every penny for six months gave us a new appreciation for money and a better understanding of where we were financially and where we wanted to go.

    I want to encourage you to take control of your finances no matter where you are at this point in your life. This information is good for anyone, especially those who are in college or just now starting a career.

CHAPTER THREE:

Job Preparation — Making a Great First Impression by Being Prepared

---

If you are a high school student, you will want to pay close attention to the next few pages. If you are a college student and not sure if you're on the right track, the next few pages may help you determine the path to pursue.

You, like most students, are excited about the reality of graduating from high school. You can't wait to get out, but when you do, the question you may ask is, "Now what?" This is a big question and one that needs to be answered correctly....by you! Success doesn't just happen; it comes from hard work and wise choices. These two traits will help you ensure future success as you explore the next chapter of your life. You have a long life ahead of you so it's important to think about how your next decisions will affect your future. The more you prepare now, the more opportunities you will have down the road.

SIMPLIFIED SUCCESS

There is no doubt you want a job that pays well and a career you will enjoy and remain in for a long time. This doesn't happen by chance. Again, it happens by working hard and making wise choices. Life is full of trade-offs. Preparing now, putting in the time, working hard and committing to a goal is not easy, but it's a requirement if you want a better life. On the other hand, if you don't prepare, or decide to take the easier route – the path of least resistance, you will reap the consequences of that decision. It may look like this: You're stuck in a low paying job and are getting passed over by everyone in your department because you don't have the requirements needed for advancement, or you bounce around from job to job hoping something better becomes available.

Once you are in this situation, climbing out is very difficult.

You owe it to yourself to explore the possibilities that await you. These possibilities come in differently wrapped gifts, one of these being education.

As I write this, our great country has just pulled out of one of the deepest recessions we have witnessed in the last 90 years. Companies that survived the economic storm have learned how to become more efficient and employ fewer people, thereby making the job market more competitive. Many college graduates are taking entry-level positions just to get their foot in the door. The job market is extremely competitive so,

You want to be at the top of your game when it's time to enter the career world.

So, what's the next step in preparing for your future?

CHAPTER THREE

Higher education! You must continue to grow your mind to be the most productive. Once you stop learning you get overlooked and assigned to the jobs nobody else wants. Higher education comes in many forms, but here I will talk briefly about four solid choices the high school graduate can consider.

Online Classes

Online learning is one form of higher education that is available. These classes are taken via the computer and can be done at your own pace, within reason. The three main advantages of on-line learning are: 1) cheaper cost, 2) flexible study times, and 3) quick completion time.

The average cost of an online class is approximately $400 per credit hour. Most of these courses are three credit hours making the total cost $1,200 for one class. A course taken online can be substantially cheaper than one taken at a traditional college. Also, the online student has no additional living expenses, therefore making this avenue an attractive choice. This educational route can also work well for adults or non-traditional students who have careers and children.

However, there are disadvantages related to this type of education and, in my opinion, they are big.

The disadvantages include; 1) no interaction with other students, 2) no class discussions or other points of view from peers, 3) no contact with teachers and professors, and 4) the absence of working with peers, professors and administrators, who help you develop life skills. Many of those considering higher education may not have the flexibility and are confined to online classes, while others may view this avenue as their only financial option for a college education. If this is you, then find ways to connect with others who are in the same situation.

Online classes offer the material and the deadlines, but it's up to you to study and meet those deadlines. Because of this freedom the process can work well if you are disciplined, but not so well if you are undisciplined. If you have a job, online classes can offer the flexibility you need while you manage your career. You must be committed, disciplined, and well organized to get it all done. My advice for you is to use online course study only when necessary. So much of your education comes from interacting with people and working through situations you face every day. As I mentioned in chapter one, life is much more rewarding and enjoyable when you do life with people. If possible, use online learning as a supplement and don't rely on it for your complete higher education.

Trade School / Vocational School

Trade school is a wonderful opportunity for those who love working with their hands and minds. These schools are literally "hands on." Here, students roll up their sleeves and go to work immediately. Trade schools don't spend time on courses like biology, algebra, geography, and the like; they spend time working on motors, chassis, and brake lines. They spend their time building and constructing, producing, and fixing. It's on the job training and students are learning a specific trade.

CHAPTER THREE

Trade schools go to the heart of teaching students job skills which can be used immediately in the workforce. Since these schools avoid the prep or introductory level classes that college demands, students can get the training they need quickly, without spending a fortune. These schools are usually 3 - 24 months in duration depending on the complexity of the career and provide some of the best-skilled training this country has ever seen.

Trade schools have a wide range of tuition costs from $3,500 per year for two-year public programs to as much as $15,000 per year for private schools. Most public trade schools have a very reasonable tuition price range of $3,500 to $7,000 per year. These schools could have a slightly higher price tag than community colleges but cost less than a four-year university.

If you are one of these students who can't bear the thought of entering a classroom for the next four years, then a trade school may be a good option for you. Do some internet searches and find a trade school you're interested in. If you know the trade school route is not for you, perhaps you may want to visit a community or technical college.

Community College / Technical College

Community and Technical Colleges are wonderful places to begin for many high school graduates and non-traditional students. There are about 1000 of these colleges scattered throughout the United States. These schools help students achieve a shorter-term education at a fraction of the cost of some four-year colleges. Community colleges are commonly referred to as "commuter colleges" because they typically don't have housing (approximately 90% do not). Most likely, there are several within an hour's drive of the community in which you live.

Community colleges mainly offer two paths of education, the Certificate/Diploma program, and the two-year Associate Degree. The Certificate/Diploma is not a degree but marks the completion of your chosen program that will help you gain employment in your field of study. These programs avoid spending time on General Education (Gen Ed) classes and go right to the heart of your chosen profession. These certificates generally require 3-12 months to complete depending on which certificate or diploma you choose to pursue. These laser focused programs are great if you know exactly what type of career you want to pursue and don't mind starting at an entry level position. They also give you a quick education and focus on the skills needed to do a specific job. The two main advantages are: 1) avoiding the Gen Ed classes by taking only the exact courses you need; and 2) the low cost of the programs. For one-year certificates, the total cost can range from $4,000 to $5,000 including tuition and books.

The other option is a two-year Associate Degree. If you are unsure about attending a four-year college or university but want to further your education, then the two-year Associate Degree program gives you a couple of nice options. This path allows you to focus on your field of study while earning your degree in any number of fields. These two-year programs require the Gen Ed curriculum but blend these

CHAPTER THREE

classes with those in your field of study. Your total cost of tuition and books will be approximately $6,200 per year, giving you a total cost of $12,400 over the two-year period. Once you have completed the two-year program and received your Associate Degree you now have two excellent options: Option one - to enter the workplace; option two – transfer to an in-state college or university.

Most community colleges have Articulation or Transfer Agreements with in-state public universities which recognize classes taken at these community colleges. This means that completed classes and hours received at the community college will transfer to a four-year, in-state university giving you two years toward a four-year degree. Here are three benefits of Articulation Agreements: **1) Guaranteed Admission** – If you meet certain criteria set forth by the university, such as completing your Associate Degree and meeting a required GPA at the community college, you would automatically be accepted into the four-year university; **2) Frozen Tuition Costs** – Many universities freeze the cost of tuition you paid during your two years at the community college and allow this price to carry over for your final two years; **3) Transfer Credits** – Don't just assume that your credits will transfer to the university. Obtain a list of required courses in your field of study from your community college, then discuss with admissions at the university to see what will transfer after you have completed your Associate Degree. **Program-to-Program Charting** is also a benefit because it shows how your completed 2-year study integrates into the bachelor's degree program.

The one question you must ask when looking for a community college: Does the college have Articulation or Transfer Agreements with any in-state college or university? If a community college does not have these agreements in place, continue your search for one that does.

Now that you are armed with an Associate Degree, you can confidently enter the work force as a college educated employee or continue your pursuit of a bachelor's degree at a four-year college or university.

Colleges/Universities

Colleges and universities come in all shapes and sizes. These establishments are found in large cities and small towns from coast to coast. These schools can range in size from less than 1,000 students to more than 50,000. There are nearly 2,600 universities in the United States that are designed around a four-year curriculum. Whereas trade schools and community colleges are considered shorter distance runs, college is more of a marathon.

You may ask, "Why go through the marathon process when I don't have to?" "Why should I have to take biology when I am going to study business management?" These are good questions and ones that I asked when I began my college career. What I eventually learned was that the college process broadened my thinking and helped me become well-rounded. Taking different courses and learning about different subjects expanded my mind. Plus, the 4 to 5-year process does two more things; it prepares you for your future career, and college living

CHAPTER THREE

prepares you for life. Many times, I heard my dad say that 50% of a student's education is inside the classroom, while 50% is learned outside the classroom. He was saying that while a classroom education is the reason students attend college, the other half of the education comes from the necessary challenges, responsibilities, and demands created by living on their own. These experiences help students prepare for basic social and life situations they will encounter every day of their lives. A college education comes in many different forms over the span of 4-5 years and these life experiences help mold students into well-rounded adults and good candidates for employers.

Now let's find out how much a four-year college education is going to cost.

Colleges and universities have higher tuition costs than the other school options that have been discussed. Four-year colleges have higher overhead costs because of the wide range of programs and services offered. The larger costs associated with four-year institutions are tuition, room, meals, and books. Let's look at some costs:

In-state public universities had a total average price tag of $23,190 for the 2019-2020 school year. Here is the breakdown; $10,440 for tuition, $11,510 for room and meals, and $1,240 for books.

Out-of-state public universities had a total average price tag of $39,570 for the same period. Here is the breakdown; $26,820 for tuition, $11,510 for room and meals, and $1,240 for books.

Private universities had an average annual price tag of $51,110 with the big difference being tuition of $36,880; room and meals averaged $12,990 while books were $1,240.

Much of the college price tag is non-negotiable, but if you are a sophomore or higher you may be able to save money on housing and meals. A large segment of students attending four-year universities either stay in university housing or rent apartments/houses just off campus. Students living off campus may be able to trim the cost of room and meals since they have more flexibility in these areas. Non-commuter freshmen are generally required to live in university provided housing which is referred to as "on campus" housing. This allows for stability as freshmen adjust to living away from home.

As we re-examine the price tags above, you can see why so many students elect to attend a public university inside their own states' border. Going out-of-state or attending a private university could add an extra $60,000 - $100,000 to the cost of a college education.

Now let's talk about how financial aid and scholarships play a huge part of the decision-making process.

Financial Aid

Financial Aid comes from four main sources, the federal government, the state government, colleges/universities, and private organizations. Types of financial aid provided by these sources consist of grants, scholarships, loans, and work-study funds. Anyone who wants to apply for any type of federal financial aid must file for the Free Application for Federal Student Aid (FAFSA).

CHAPTER THREE

Let's look at the four types of aid that these sources provide:

Grants – A grant is money that does not have to be repaid. These may be need-based, merit-based or student specific and are offered by the federal and state governments as well as some higher learning institutions. The competition for these is high because this money does not have to be repaid. The federal government offers the following grants:

- **Pell Grants** – for undergraduate students who demonstrate a financial need; also based on the cost of the school.

- **Federal Supplemental Education Opportunity Grants** – for undergraduate students who demonstrate a strong financial need; administered by financial offices of participating colleges.

- **Teacher Education Assistance for College and Higher Education Grants** – TEACH grants are for those planning to teach school in high-need fields and low-income areas.

- **Iraq and Afghanistan Service Grants** – for students whose parent or guardian died during military service in Iraq or Afghanistan.

Loans – These are offered by both the federal government and colleges/universities. The word "loan" means you must pay the money back along with interest. Loans give you immediate access to funds and the ability, in some cases, to defer payment until you graduate. There are several loans available for college students and they include:

- **Subsidized Loans** – for students who demonstrate a financial need; loan payments are deferred.

- **Unsubsidized Loans** – for students regardless of financial need; loan payments are not deferred.

- **PLUS Loans** – for graduate or professional students and parents of dependent undergraduate students not covered by other financial aid options.

- **Perkins Loans** – for students with extreme financial need; these are provided to graduate or undergraduate students by the institution.

- **Bank Loans** – for any student; loan payments are not deferred; receiving credit depends on your ability to borrow and rates could be higher.

Please do your research before automatically committing to any of these loans. While it's easy to borrow money, it's often more difficult to pay it back. From my banker point of view, I have seen many young people destroy their credit/credit score by not being prudent in borrowing/repaying. Again, please be careful and ask questions before signing on the dotted line for any type of loan.

Work-Study – This program allows you to work and earn money for college. Work-study programs provide students with federally funded jobs typically at the school in which they are enrolled. This could be a job at the library, at a residence hall or as a custodian. There are many jobs for which you can apply and there is a wide variety of positions and pay offered.

CHAPTER THREE

Scholarships

Full-tuition scholarships are considered the pinnacle of college scholarships. These prizes cover a major portion of college expenses over a four-year period. Since these scholarships are so coveted and limited, the competition is very strong. Applications for these scholarships are readily available online or by contacting the college directly.

Academic or merit-based scholarships are also readily available for application if you have met the academic standards that are required. Most colleges have certain criteria based on ACT or SAT scores and high school GPA. Schools also look at community service and time volunteered to distinguish one candidate from another. A well-prepared application, high GPA and aptitude test scores, and community service should command the attention of most universities.

Local scholarships are funded by businesses, foundations, and organizations in your community. These will generally range from $250-$5,000 with some being higher. The best place to learn about these scholarships is from your high school guidance counselor. Some of these scholarships will be based slightly more on need but organizations will examine your academics and community service very closely and determine recipients based on the total body of work.

Your high school counselor can also guide you to state-funded scholarships that reward graduating seniors for educational excellence in the classroom and for high ACT and SAT exam scores. These scholarship amounts differ by state, but any amount received can be a big help.

Additionally, several corporate and foundation scholarships can cover the tuition cost of a four-year degree. These are generally awarded annually requiring the student to meet certain academic standards each year. These awards tend to have strong merit and need-based requirements.

There are thousands of books and websites that are available to you as you go through this process. Two of the websites I found helpful are www.collegescholarships.org and www.scholarships.com. These and others can give you an in-depth education on funds available for higher education.

Of course, you have much work to do and many decisions to make. But as you progress through the maze of higher education decisions, you will begin to determine which path is best for you. Now that you are prepared with either a certificate or degree, you have something desirable to market - yourself and your higher education!

Now it's time to polish the package by writing a great cover letter and resume.

Cover Letter and Resume

Your resume and cover letter may be the first item about you that many potential employers see. First, do your research on the company. Find out all you can about it by doing internet searches. If you are close to someone on the inside, try to gain as much knowledge as you can to set you apart from other applicants. This will help you customize your information to the company's need and help you stand out from your

CHAPTER THREE

competition.

Make sure all information on your cover letter and resume is correct and neat. Also, you must address the letter to the right person, or the one who will give you the best chance of getting it to the right person. If you don't know and can't find the name of the person you should address it to specifically, mention a title and department, such as "Dear Software Team Hiring Manager." Avoid the use of "To Whom It May Concern" as this is an old-fashioned salutation.

Cover Letter

Your cover letter is an introduction of yourself to someone you may have never met. This is a one-page letter that is straight to the point. Your cover letter will need to address five items: 1) greeting, 2) opening, 3) hook, 4) skills, and 5) closing. These 4-5 paragraphs will be no longer than one page in total and in the range of 250-350 words. This document should flow easily from one paragraph to another in a story-like manner.

The **greeting** is your introduction to the company to which you are applying. The **opening** is a personable, inviting paragraph that highlights your skills and how these would be an excellent match for the position. Remember, you are selling a product, and that product is YOU!

The **hook** is where you want to highlight your past achievements as they relate to the job for which you are applying. If you are a recent graduate and have little or no previous work experience, then you should list accomplishments you have achieved in your college or trade school career. Dawn Calvert, a former manager at IBM, says one of the first things she looked for in an applicant was any leadership role or other involvement in high school or college activities which demonstrated that person's leadership capabilities. This is usually a good indicator of determination and drive and the ability to manage multiple tasks like going to school and working. She would also pay close attention to any type of awards or recognitions they may have received. Knowing they were the treasurer of their sorority, or that they set the record for selling the most tablets in a single weekend at Best Buy, would tell her much about the work ethic of the individual. This is where you want to "hook" your audience.

Next you want to address your **skills**. If you have prior job experiences which required certain skills, you will want to give a short explanation for those. Only list those which add value and pertain to the job for which you are applying. You may have had a job that required a specific skill, one that demanded an early arrival or one that was physically challenging. The challenges listed here show that you are skillful in a certain area, dependable, and not afraid of hard work. The more of these characteristics you can highlight, the better picture your potential employer will have of you. You want to toot your horn but beware of using such adjectives as "dynamic, great, tremendous" throughout the entire cover letter. These and other similar words are subjective and can be counterproductive if used too frequently. If an adjective describes you well, then use it. Be factual and don't exaggerate. Be careful not to insert irrelevant fluff in your cover letter as this will diminish the attributes and skills already mentioned.

CHAPTER THREE

The right information written the right way can be an enjoyable reading experience for your potential employer and make a great first impression.

The **closing** should be a summation of what you can offer the company. It should only be three sentences long which includes the summation, your contact information and a thank you. It is important to thank him/her for taking the time to read your letter and let him/her know you are looking forward to learning more about this opportunity.

The Resume

Your resume should be typed without errors and contain only accurate and truthful information. The truth will always come out at some point, so don't ever put yourself in a damaging situation. Even if you are doing a good job, the chances of your being fired are almost certain if you were hired under false pretenses. Honesty is always the best policy.

You should keep your resume to one page if you have limited or no work experience. If a company is looking for an experienced person, they are not likely to hire you anyway so be precise and brief. Don't put irrelevant information on your resume. This will be detected immediately and give the employer a reason to put yours aside and pick up the next one.

Keep your resume simple and clean looking, avoiding clutter and distractions. Be careful with color and fonts as too much of this will distract the reader. Once you have a format you like, you are now ready to begin the process of putting it together.

Below are the six items you need to include on your resume:

Name and Contact Information:

At the top of your resume, put your full name and a professional looking email address. Next is your phone number and street address. The one big exception: If you're applying for a job in another state, consider leaving your address off.

Summary Paragraph: Address these items in an easy to read paragraph:

- Work ethic
- Years of experience
- Position held for your previous employer
- Skills you can bring to the company in the role for which you are applying
- Highest degree of education

The summary paragraph should grab the attention of the reader and make him/her want to continue.

Employment History:

Usually you should only list jobs where you stayed the longest. Longevity shows commitment and gives the employer one more reason to hire you. However, if you had a short-term job that required a specific skill, you may want to list this especially if that skill pertains to the job for which you are applying. If you have limited work experience, then list all jobs. Make sure you list any internships in this category as well. If you have absolutely ZERO work experience, you will have to take Employment History out of your resume and move Education to #3.

Your employment information should be in the top half

CHAPTER THREE

of the resume to make sure the reader does not have to scroll down to see it. You should place your previous jobs in chronological order (most recent first), and list job titles, company names, and start/end dates of each.

Place 2-4 bullet points under each job or activity explaining what you did. Don't just talk about job duties, state what you accomplished. Did you exceed established goals during the year or were you the top salesperson during a sales campaign? These show not only what you did, but *how* you did. It is important to highlight these work-related accomplishments and market yourself in the best manner possible using the correct words efficiently.

Skills:

This is the next section for your resume; where you list relevant skills associated with the job you're applying for. Don't just list anything and everything. Think about what will be required to do the job. Does it require leadership, problem solving, heavy lifting, customer service or technical skills? Think about it and tailor this portion of your resume to make it dove-tail with your cover letter and the job you're seeking. Any specific examples that show how you integrated your skill set into previous jobs and activities will give the reader a better idea of who you are and what you are able to do for his/her company. Also, think about key words, such as those mentioned above, and insert them in your resume so you can get through online job application systems.

Education:

This is where you put the name of your school(s), your field of study, and graduation date. Again, just like the employment section, your education should be listed in chronological order. If you're in high school or college, it's assumed that you completed Junior High, so this shouldn't be listed. However, if you are in college or have just graduated, you should list your high school to show your levels of progression and where you're from. Your next item will be your GPA. If you had a GPA above 3.0 then list it here. If it was below a 3.0, then consider excluding it from your resume.

Community Involvement: If you've participated in any volunteer work or helped in your community in other ways, this is the section for those good deeds. You can list the location, dates worked, and the work contributed. Your involvement should be clearly stated so the employer realizes you are working towards your career, a college scholarship or to make your community a better place to live. These works may satisfy an employer if you haven't had prior employment. If you haven't done any volunteer work, just leave this section off your resume.

Achievements, accomplishments, and awards do not need a separate page but are great items to list. You can work these in as needed into the body of your resume underneath the categories above. After you have completed your resume, proofread it very carefully and ask someone else to do the same. Make sure your paragraphs flow well and the information listed pertains to the job you are seeking.

The Prelude to the Interview

You have cleared the first hurdle – you received a call back! Your cover letter and resume gave you the opportunity

CHAPTER THREE

to get the interview you were hoping for. This is where your social skills will help you through the interviewing process. There are a few social skills that are essential when you are preparing for your interview. They are punctuality, presentation, respect, and manners.

Punctuality – You should always arrive early. Leave yourself enough time in case you get caught in traffic, have a flat tire or any other unseen emergency. Showing up late for an interview shows a lack of respect for the interviewer and the company. This is your chance to make a great first impression and being late is a deal breaker.

Presentation – Your attire should be customized for the job you are pursuing. If you are a man applying for a position at a bank, you should dress in a suit and tie, while a woman should wear a pant suit, dress or skirt and blouse. If you are interviewing for field work at a construction company, you may want to dress in khakis and a nice button-down shirt, maybe a tie, depending on what you have learned about the company. You don't want to underdress, but you don't want to overdress either.

If you have body art, as in tattoos or piercings, it should not show. Tattoos should be covered up completely and jewelry from piercings should be taken out, except for traditional ear piercings. You may say, "That's not fair." The fact is the company's management staff will hire those applicants who will best represent their company and its values. Visible tattoos and piercings could be the things that keep you from getting the job.

Grooming also falls into this category. Being clean and well-groomed is expected. Hair should be combed or brushed, men should be clean shaven or facial hair neatly trimmed, body should be clean, and fingernails trimmed. Since being well-groomed is expected, you won't get additional points, but it will greatly increase your chances for employment if you are.

Respect – At all times, you will give everyone with whom you come in contact, RESPECT. It's "Yes ma'am," or "No sir," as you look the interviewer in the eye, especially when she/he speaks and when you answer questions. A firm handshake and eye contact are non-verbal communication skills that say much about who you are. These actions show your confidence and your respect for the interviewer.

Manners – Good manners go hand in hand with respect. During your visit, look for ways to show your consideration. Always remember to address your elders with "Mr." or "Ms.", "Yes sir" or "No ma'am," whatever the circumstance dictates. Opening a door or holding a chair for someone may be the small item that gets you recognized. Remember, the little things could be the difference in you landing the job or someone else getting the call.

The categories above can be summed up in these four points:

1) Presentation is everything
2) Do what is right
3) Remain humble
4) Treat others as you would want to be treated

Doing what is right shows that you consider other people's feelings and genuine humility is attractive to any person, organization, or company. These traits are essential parts of presentation.

CHAPTER THREE

The Interview

The four characteristics (punctuality, presentation, respect, and manners) should always stand out. These show your character, humility, and respect for others. If these are present, you have an opportunity to get through the interview with flying colors. One more piece of information that is particularly important, and we briefly mentioned it before, is that you have done your research and are knowledgeable about the company, firm, or person who is interviewing you. When you have done your homework and have knowledge of the company, you will be much more confident when speaking to the interviewer. You want to be confident, but careful about being overly confident or worse, arrogant. The right amount of confidence coupled with the four characteristics mentioned above, make an attractive employee. This type of employee can generally work with anyone in any type of situation.

Also, by gaining knowledge of the company, you are showing your level of interest. You are telling the person, "I care about this interview, and I am willing to do what it takes to make sure you gain a great employee." Do the things that other people don't do. Go the extra mile because this is the effort you must put forth to have a chance at getting the position. There are other hungry, young people in the job market who are pursuing the same position and one or more of them will do the little extra to get noticed.

Competition is tough, so you should prepare yourself thoroughly and give the decision makers no choice but to hire you.

The Greeting

This may be the first time you have ever met the interviewer; that's how it happened for me as I prepared to interview for the bank position.

Mr. Smith, the Bank President, was looking for someone who would represent his company well. He was looking for someone who was on time, made a good presentation and one who showed respect and manners. I was about to make a first impression on the man who had the power to hire me and I wanted to make sure it was a good one.

Thankfully, my father taught my siblings and me the way to make a great first impression by following the steps outlined in this book. These are the coaching steps my dad gave me the night before my interview:

"It is vital that you greet Mr. Smith with warm eye contact and a smile. This shows confidence and a good self-image. A smile keeps you relaxed as you enter the room. As you approach him, he will most likely introduce himself and extend his hand. You are to do the same. He will be looking for two things in this greeting: eye to eye contact and, a firm handshake. Always refer to him as "Mr." unless he permits you to call him by his first name. If you are offered a drink or snack, politely say, "No thank you." When seated, stay relaxed but sit tall with shoulders back and hands in lap. This posture shows attentiveness and respect."

CHAPTER THREE

Keys to a Successful Interview

Dad continued: "At this point, you are ready to be interviewed. He will most likely ask you to take a seat, and the interview will begin. He will have preselected questions to find out as much as possible about you in a short amount of time. Most likely you are not the only interviewee, so the first interview will be brief. Usually, first interviews are no more than one hour. After these initial interviews are completed, he will separate the candidates into two groups, one that will get a call back for a second interview, and one that won't."

"Be truthful and candid and do not give one-word answers to his questions."

"He will ask questions leading you to expand on experiences you have had in previous jobs and activities. Expand on these, but once you have answered the question satisfactorily, be quiet. Saying too much is as bad as not saying enough."

"Some of these questions will revolve around teamwork and how well you get along with your co-workers. Other questions will probe deeply into how you react to certain situations and how well you handle these."

"Employers are looking for employees who work well with others; those who don't let disagreements interfere with their work and those who leave their personal problems at home."

"If Mr. Smith asks for questions, be ready to respond. Your questions should be about the job or the company. Again, this shows your attentiveness and your eagerness to learn more about this opportunity."

"Above all, be yourself. Don't try to be somebody you aren't. If you aren't the person he's looking for, then it's not the right fit for either of you. The hiring must work for both parties or it won't work at all. Just be yourself. If you are hired, Mr. Smith knows he is hiring the person who was interviewed and not one who performed the part."

"When the interview is over, show Mr. Smith sincere appreciation for the opportunity. He has taken his valuable time to talk with you and your appreciation should show."

Remember, if you don't get the job, it's not the end of the world. Just continue to apply the lessons you have learned, and the right job will come along, maybe when you least expect it.

CHAPTER FOUR:

Physical Health — You Only Get One Shot

The Importance of a Healthy Diet

A healthy body is a blessing most of us take for granted especially when we're young. God made our bodies to be self-sufficient and to function in amazing ways. You can do an internet search on "facts about the human body" and find all kinds of interesting information most of us never knew about our bodies. The body is a finely tuned machine and is designed to stay that way if we take care of it. Therefore, it's important to understand that what we put into our bodies will have either a positive or negative effect on our overall health.

Isn't it amazing that the worst tasting foods are the ones that are best for us? When I was young, my sister, two brothers and I would sit around the dinner table and hear our parents say, "Eat your vegetables, they're good for you!" With disgusting and anxious looks on our faces, we would load up our forks, hold our noses and begin chewing as fast as we could, swallowing as quickly as possible without choking, then chasing it with several gulps of milk to wash out the taste! This didn't happen every night, but it did happen often. We were required to eat our vegetables and all the other healthy foods Mom put on our plates. Little did I know this would help me form good eating habits throughout my adult life and train me to do the same for my daughter.

Obesity is the number one health problem in our society for kids under 18 years of age. Parents, we are responsible for our children's health and the more quickly we begin to form good eating habits, so will our children. When we put healthier food on the table, the habit of healthy eating can be formed. This is a good time to tell you I am not a doctor, dietician, nor do I have any medical background. These are just choices that have worked for me.

So, let's talk about some of the healthy foods we can start with to help us form good eating habits.

Healthy Snacks - Fruits / Vegetables/ Nuts

It seems like I'm always running into some of my friends at work or the gym and sometimes the topic of staying fit comes up. Many times, I have heard (and have said it myself), "If I didn't snack at night, I could lose weight." In reality, it's probably not the late-night snacking that is the culprit, *but what I choose to snack on.* Sometimes, I'll go for the ice cream or leftover dessert when I could have eaten a piece of fresh fruit or a handful of nuts. For me, it's about making a conscious effort and doing two things: 1) making sure I have

CHAPTER FOUR

healthy snacks on hand and 2) choosing the healthy option. Do I go for the candy or the fresh fruit? Thanks to Christy, who is an excellent shopper, I don't have much junk food in the pantry, so I usually pick the fresh fruit or nuts; and it's my opinion that these are better than candy. Bananas, navel oranges, red grapefruit, seedless grapes, raisins, mangos, peaches, watermelon, apples, cashews, almonds - the list is endless. We get in our minds that because these foods are healthy, they don't taste as good as sweets. This couldn't be further from the truth. Fruit, nuts and vegetables are some of nature's "candy" and the best choices for healthy snacking!

I would like to challenge you to go out and find a few of these nutritional items and put away the cupcakes, candy bars, and soft drinks for a week and snack on nothing except fruits, veggies, nuts, and water. Your taste buds may have to adjust a little, but once you begin to enjoy the different taste, you will be coming back for more. Not only have you given your taste buds a break from all the junk food, you have given your body a break as well. Our bodies are designed to eliminate small amounts of bad foods over time, but it has a more difficult time doing this if we continually ingest these types of foods.

Now let's talk about some ideas and entrees that can make a nutritional difference for you and your family.

Breakfast Foods

We have found it works well for our family to have a set schedule for breakfast during the week. A little planning by Christy has taken away the stress in the morning and gives

Micah some input as to what she would like to eat. This is the way we do it.

Our family sits down and chooses five healthy breakfast meals (one for each day of the school week) and we stick with this all year long. "Wow, that's pretty restrictive," you say. Well, maybe so, but remember Micah is helping to create the menu, so she is able to choose five different healthy breakfasts that she enjoys. Sure, we vary from this some, but this is generally our plan. (You may find other healthy breakfast ideas by searching websites such as Pinterest, and you may choose to rotate ten breakfast ideas).

Planning ahead like this accomplishes three things; 1) it eliminates the stress of trying to find something your children will eat before heading to school, 2) it gives you comfort that your children are eating something good before they walk out the door, and 3) it allows you to prepare beforehand and have all the breakfast items stocked and ready. Once you and your children adapt to this pattern, it becomes a habit and simplifies your lives. It also makes for enjoyable and stress-free mornings. This plan can be implemented anytime, but the younger your children are, the easier it will be to adapt. Take the step to help your children form good eating habits that will last the rest of their lives. You can find thousands of good, easy ideas right on your computer. Your only limit is your imagination and the amount of effort you decide to put into it.

Main Courses

I must admit that my family likes to sit down to a good, old-fashioned country dinner a few nights each month. When

CHAPTER FOUR

Christy tells us that we will be having meatloaf with the sweet ketchup sauce, mashed potatoes, and green beans, I want to shut down my computer, go home early and help her get it ready! Yes, it is a very tasty meal and one we eat about once a month, but it's not the best meal for our bodies.

So, let's get back to our healthy meal challenge. Christy, who is a stay-at-home mom, used the Pinterest website to find healthy foods we could eat and hopefully enjoy. She found some dishes that sounded good, so she gave them a try. We couldn't believe how good they were! Some of these dishes were so good that we have decided to add them to our favorites. The goal here is to find other healthy meals to mix in with your favorites. My point is, there are good, healthy options out there for you and your family and all it takes is some experimentation to find those you and your family will enjoy.

Moderation is the Key

Many people do life at 90 miles an hour all the time! They don't take the time to eat right because they are always on the go. Whether it's business or taking care of the family, some believe they have no time to worry about eating right or at the right times. Eating poor foods at the wrong times will drain the energy and stamina your body needs to perform at a high level. Look at it this way; the wrong food in your body is like the wrong fuel in your car. It may run for a little while but eventually it will spit and sputter and eventually stop running.

Keep your energy and stamina at high levels by eating the proper foods, in proper quantities, at the proper times.

Moderation is a good rule of thumb for most areas of your life, especially in the area of food consumption. We all enjoy food and we should, just not too much of it. Having some restraint at the dinner table can add years to your life and help you eliminate many of the diseases that come with obesity, including heart issues, clogged arteries, diabetes, and many others.

Obesity is a silent killer. Many of us don't think much about it until it's too late. It has become a way of life for far too many Americans. It is important to start your children on healthy, correctly portioned meals when they are young. This becomes a way of life for you and your family and sets the tone for healthy eating habits over time.

Again, it takes commitment on your part as the parent, and the ability to stick to this plan until the habit is formed. Once this lifestyle change has been implemented, you have set the stage for healthy eating habits for your future and theirs.

Exercise

As you begin to see the weight fall off because of your healthy eating choices, this progress may give you the motivation to begin some form of exercise. If you are one who exercises on a regular basis, you probably began with an easier routine at first and added exercises to your repertoire as you built up stamina. Maybe you began by walking for fifteen minutes around your neighborhood. You eventually built this up to thirty minutes or an hour and then possibly started

CHAPTER FOUR

jogging. Once you saw the positive effects it had on your body, it gave you the motivation and excitement to try other, more demanding exercises like running or lifting weights.

The goal is to find something that increases your heart rate and gives you muscle tone. The list is endless and again, is only limited by your imagination. Exercise doesn't have to be hard, but it should be consistent to help you achieve the healthy results you desire. Clear any exercise program with your doctor first, then get started and stick with it.

Drink Water

When you drink water, good things happen for you. It is absolutely the best drink for your body and your wallet. To begin with, your body is already comprised of approximately 60% water, so it makes sense that water is the best drink for your body. Here are four benefits you enjoy when you choose to drink water: 1) It keeps you hydrated by replenishing fluids your body has excreted, 2) It dilutes and flushes impurities out of your system, 3) It helps burn calories since your body has to expend energy to heat the water and, 4) It costs much less than soft drinks and has zero calories! You just have to create the habit. Water, as your main drink, is the hands down winner to take care of your body and your budget!

We've talked about some positive things that can benefit your health, now let's talk about some things you should avoid.

Tobacco Use

Tobacco use is still very much a part of our society. Whether it comes in the form of cigarettes, cigars, or other forms of smokeless tobacco, it is common and accessible. Unfortunately, too many young people get their hands on some form of tobacco at a young age. Many are not taught the dangers associated with tobacco and fall in with the crowd as they begin to experiment early in their lives. They think it's cool or "grown up" to have a cigarette dangling from their lips or a "pinch of snuff" between their cheek and gums. This is sad to see because many young people don't understand that these actions form habits. These habits form lifestyles and lifestyles determine our successes and failures in many different aspects of our lives. Picking up one cigarette could put you on the path to smoking two packs a day for sixty years! That same cigarette could lead you to a life filled with lung problems, developing diseases such as cancer and Chronic Obstructive Pulmonary Disease (C.O.P.D.).

I once knew a man who began smoking at a young age. He was a kid back in the 1950's and scientists had not come out with any scientific information about the dangers of tobacco. Many people smoked or "chewed," and tobacco was an accepted part of society. There were very few "No Smoking" signs around. People smoked on airplanes, in restaurants, in office buildings, pretty much anywhere. It was accepted. Anyway, this kid grew up and continued to smoke throughout his adult life. As public awareness came out about the dangers of smoking, he tried to quit but he couldn't. He

CHAPTER FOUR

was hooked. Over time, he continued to fight it, but the urge always brought him back. Over time extensive damage was done to his lungs and he developed C.O.P.D. Gradually, his lungs began to fill with fluid, which had to be drained constantly. He eventually died a slow, painful death at the age of 72. This man had a family heritage of ancestors who lived well into their 90's. He most likely had these same genes and the possibility of a longer and healthier life, but one day he picked up a cigarette and it changed his life forever.

How sad this can happen. How quickly this can happen! Do yourself a favor. Don't touch tobacco! If you have already fallen into the lifestyle, get help and get it now. The longer you go, the harder it is to quit.

Drugs

Unfortunately, narcotics or drugs are also a part of our society, although unlike tobacco, they are illegal and therefore, concealed. Whether drugs come in the form of marijuana, pills, steroids, or harder substances such as heroin and cocaine, all are addictive and extremely dangerous. Not only will these substances cause significant health problems, but they could give you an early funeral!

Drugs are everywhere even though few people see them. The underground market is alive and lurking in places you never suspect. Pushers or sellers of narcotics live among us, but we see nothing. Some are targeting our young people hoping to gain them as customers thereby expanding their client base and their cash flow. Some sellers even package harmful drugs in colorful cartoon packages that look like candy and give them to kids! This is a sickening reality but one we must be aware of and discuss with our children.

Alcohol

Alcohol, like tobacco, is quite common in our society. It is legal to purchase if you are of legal age and it is widely accepted in today's world. Alcohol has been a part of our world ever since it began. Alcohol has become a multi-billion-dollar business and sales continue to increase year after year. You can find it on most supermarket and drugstore shelves and find it cheap. Alcohol can be found at many family gatherings, social activities, or parties. Alcohol is common throughout our society because of the effect it has on people. It tends to help you relax making it acceptable in social situations. It "loosens you up" and allows you to relax in conversation. Many people are not comfortable in social situations unless they are in a relaxed state of mind, and frankly, alcohol can do this for you.

But this is where the trouble can start.

The problem with alcohol is not the alcohol itself, but the decisions made by the one consuming the alcohol. Many people don't know when to stop drinking. Once they become relaxed and begin to enjoy the party, they continue to drink. The more they drink, the more their judgment becomes impaired and problems are more likely to happen. Once the moderation line is crossed, they become a danger to themselves and others.

I know this is a sensitive subject and one many of you

CHAPTER FOUR

have discussed with your families. In my opinion, taking a drink of alcohol is not wrong, however each person must ask him/herself, "What is my motivation for drinking?" Is it a glass of wine to spark the romance in a beautiful marriage or is it a fifth of whiskey to attempt to drown out the pain? Regardless of how you answer this question, you must realize that consuming any amount of alcohol could open the door to potential problems. The problem with the word "moderation" is that it can be defined differently by everyone. When alcohol begins to control a person and infringe on someone else's turf, it then becomes an issue. Even deeper, if alcohol begins to control a person's thoughts and emotions, it begins to control the person's life and the issue escalates into a much larger problem.

Alcohol has affected many lives and families negatively. These people didn't set out to destroy their lives with alcohol, but it happened just the same. They may have had an addictive personality and one taste got them hooked. They may have just wanted to experiment and see what it was all about. But just like that cigarette or drug, they were hooked from the first taste and could never turn back. The older you are the more you have seen this story play out in families all over. If you have never tasted alcohol, don't start. Don't cave-in to peer pressure just to fit in with the crowd, and avoid situations that make you uncomfortable. This could make you the outcast with one group but allow you to find true friends who share the same core values. If you choose to socialize with alcohol, please do so responsibly for yourself, your family, and the others around you.

    Your body and your good health are wonderful gifts from God. If you treat your body well, it will serve you well. Your body is made to last a long time and is designed to make sure you get the most out of it. You were put on this earth for a purpose, and much of your purpose is to help others. Your good health will go a long way in making this happen!

CHAPTER FIVE:

Spiritual Health — Your Eternity Depends Upon It

[This section is based on Christian principles from the historical book — The Holy Bible. Any biblical interpretation or reference I've given in this book is based on my belief of the scriptures.]

The Bible tells us that we are all created by God, in His image (Genesis 1:27). God created mankind and in us He placed a desire, a void that can only be filled by Him. He created us to have a relationship with Him and to save us from the sin in this world. John 3:16 says "God so loved the world, that He gave us His only Son, that everyone who believes in Him, will not perish, but have eternal life."

In the Old Testament, God's law stated that each time a sin was committed, something had to be sacrificed or put to death before the sinner could be forgiven. The sacrifice was an animal, maybe a lamb or sheep, cow, or calf from the herd of the one who sinned. Definitely a deterrent, because losing a member of the herd meant losing money.

In the New Testament gospels of Matthew, Mark, Luke and John, God's divine plan is revealed: The birth of His son, Jesus, into this sinful world where He would grow up and eventually begin His ministry.

However, God's plan took it one step further.

God knew when His son was born, He would eventually die on a cross as the ultimate sacrifice for our past, present, and future sins. God knew only the *perfect* sacrifice could cover the multitude of sin in this world. That perfect sacrifice would be the one person in this world who never sinned…Jesus.

John 3:16 tells us that we must believe in Jesus Christ to have eternal life. In John 14:6 Jesus says, "I am the way, the truth, and the life. No one can come to the Father except through Me." These scriptures are referring to you and me accepting Jesus Christ as our Lord and Savior. So, when we die and go to our eternal destination, it will be with Him in heaven. The Bible tells us in John 3:3 we must be born again. This obviously doesn't mean physical birth but spiritual birth; at the point when we ask Jesus to come and live in our hearts.

You may ask, "What happens if I don't receive Jesus as my Savior?" According to the bible, if you have not invited Jesus to live in your heart, you will be banished from Him once you die. Romans 6:23 says "For the wages of sin is death but the free gift of God is eternal life through Christ Jesus our Lord." This scripture is speaking of spiritual death meaning you will not live with Him forever in paradise unless you receive the free gift of eternal life. John 3:36 says "All who believe in God's son have eternal life. Those who don't obey the Son will never experience eternal life, but the wrath of God remains upon them." 2 Thessalonians 1:8-9 says "He (Jesus) will come with his mighty angels....bringing destruction on those who don't know God and on those who refuse to obey the Good News of our Lord Jesus. They will be punished with everlasting destruction, forever separated from the Lord and from His glorious presence." These are harsh words indeed, but only for those who haven't received Jesus. Just a few paragraphs below I have included the prayer of salvation which you can pray and become a child of God.

Many people believe the Bible is true, but don't read it. We must read the Bible to know how we are to live our lives. The Bible is our life manual – our blueprint or road map. Studying the Bible and obeying what it says are major components in establishing a relationship with God. In Matthew 7:21 Jesus says "Not all people who sound religious are really godly. They may refer to Me as Lord, but they won't enter the Kingdom of Heaven. The decisive issue is whether they obey My Father in heaven." So, we must not only believe in Jesus, we must read and obey God's word.

Forgiveness and Salvation

Receiving Jesus as your Lord is as easy as A-B-C. I first heard this easy-to-remember acronym from my former pastor, Harry B. Jones.

First, you must ADMIT you have sinned. Romans 3:23 says, "For all have sinned; all fall short of God's glorious standard." Mankind is born into sin and it's only through Jesus that we become redeemed. Romans 3:10 says, "No one is good

— not even one," meaning we are all sinners and need redemption through Jesus.

Secondly, you must BELIEVE. Romans 10:9 states "If you confess with your mouth that Jesus is Lord and believe in your heart that God raised Him from the dead, you will be saved." You must believe Jesus was born and lived on this earth and eventually died for your sins. Again, John 3:16 says "For God so loved the world that He gave us His only son, that everyone who believes in Him will not perish but have eternal life."

The C stands for COMMIT. John 8:12 says "When Jesus spoke to the people, He said, "I am the light of the world. If you follow me, you won't be stumbling through the darkness, because you will have the light that leads to life." Agree to commit your life to Christ and begin living the way He wants you to.

You can pray this simple prayer right now: "Father, I admit that I am a sinner and I believe you sent your son Jesus to die on the cross for my sins. Jesus, I am asking you to come and live inside my heart. I commit my life to you and agree to obey and follow you. In Jesus' name, amen."

Once you have prayed this prayer, you are a child of God! You are a forgiven and clean person because you have invited Jesus to come and live in your heart. It's His Holy Spirit who is alive in your heart.

In Acts 2, when Jesus ascended into heaven, He told His disciples He would send His Holy Spirit to them. His Holy Spirit inhabits the hearts of those who have invited Him in. This is God's salvation plan for the world. Once you have given your

CHAPTER FIVE

life to Christ, you will want to stay in close contact with Him daily. *The ways to do this are through prayer, Bible reading, and going to church.*

Prayer and Meditation

Prayer is an amazing concept developed by God. Prayer is our life line or our phone line to God and to get to know Him, we must pray. But how do we, as imperfect people, engage with a perfect God? We are sinners and He is perfect, so how can He hear our prayers when they are coming from imperfect creatures?

We, *on our own merit*, have no standing before God; therefore, we *must* come before Him in the name of His son, Jesus Christ. Jesus Christ is the perfect go-between or the perfect conduit who allows us to connect with God through prayer. Jesus is the One who covers our sin, which is washed away when we invite Him to come and live in our hearts.

Now, when God looks at us, He sees Jesus, not us.

When we come before God in prayer, we must acknowledge we are coming to Him in the name of Jesus. When we do, God can hear our prayers. In John 14:13-14, Jesus says, "You can ask for anything *in my name*, and I will do it, because the work of the Son brings glory to the Father. Yes, ask anything *in my name* and I will do it!" Coming to God in the name of Jesus is the *first key* to God hearing our prayers.

We've discussed how to come before God when we are about to pray; how to set the table for our prayers to be heard. Now, it makes sense that God tells us somewhere in the bible *how* to pray.

In Matthew 6:9-13, God gives us instructions on how we should pray. This scripture is called "The Lord's Prayer." The Lord's Prayer is universal, and millions upon millions have memorized it. This is the New English Version that was adopted by the Church of England in 1977:

Our Father, in heaven, hallowed is your name.
Your kingdom come your will be done on earth as it is in heaven.
Give us today our daily bread,
And forgive us of our sins as we forgive those who sin against us.
Lead us not into temptation but deliver us from evil.
(For yours is the kingdom, the power and the glory forever, Amen.)

What powerful words indeed! The Lord has now given us the <u>second key</u> to the secret of Him hearing our prayers! Now, let's break it down as to what this prayer means:

"Our Father, in heaven, hallowed is your name." When you begin your prayer with these words, you are acknowledging to whom you are praying and that you are honoring God by coming to Him. This is where you want to think about how great God is, how awesome He is and thank Him for how much He has done for you. The word hallowed carries a strong sense of reverence and respect. Other words that come to mind; almighty, creator, perfect, sovereign, holy, worthy, solemn, greatness, worship, and awe just to name a few. During this time of reflection, ask God to soften your heart and

CHAPTER FIVE

to remind you of all the things He has done for you. This will prepare your heart for worshiping Him.

"Your kingdom come your will be done on earth as it is in heaven." Here you are praying He fills the hearts of His people and that His will be done through His people on earth just as His will is done in heaven. His will *is* your destiny and He desires that you fulfill it. You are praying that His goodness, mercy, and favor are unleashed on His people and this love spreads to every Christian on earth. You are also praying for those who have not yet invited Jesus to live in their hearts, praying He will soften their hearts and they will receive Him as their Lord and Savior so they can experience His love as well.

Notice the first two lines of the Lord's Prayer focus on Him while the last three lines focus on us. (We will discuss the sixth line later.) It is important that we begin our prayer by acknowledging His greatness and that His will be done. We are giving Him the respect and honor He deserves, while keeping our motives in check.

"Give us today our daily bread." This part of scripture is not only speaking of actual food, but also about spiritual food. You are asking, "Lord, give me what I need today to follow through with your will. Let your Holy Spirit guide me down the path you have for me today. Put me in contact with those who need me and those I need."

This is also where your requests come in. He wants you to ask for guidance because this shows your maturity and your desire for His will to be done above yours. He also wants you to ask Him for your personal needs. Pray for the needs of your family and friends, healing for your body, help with work issues, stressful situations, broken relationships, and whatever else you need.

You must understand God loves you more than anything and He desires to give you what you need and want when it lines up with His will. God is not Santa Claus, nor should He be treated as such, but as you pray with the right heart, God hears your prayers and answers them in His timing, not yours. Matthew 6:33 says, "Your heavenly Father....will give you all you need from day to day if you live for Him and make the Kingdom of God your primary concern." You can also find a similar passage in Luke 12:31.

Notice, He promises to provide for your needs day to day, not wants. He desires for you to have your wants, but He desires more for you to pray for His will to be done. Answers to these prayers may come quickly, but then again they may not! Let me tell you a personal story about Christy and me.

Christy and I were married in 1985, and both of us had started our careers. We wanted to get our financial feet under us, so our plan was to wait five years before starting a family. We started trying to have a baby in 1990, and we had no success. We went to the doctor to make sure there was nothing wrong, and in the meantime, we kept trying. All this time, or at least for the first 4-5 years, we were praying that God would bless us with a baby. We couldn't understand why this was happening. We believed that having a child was part of His plan for us; but still, no baby. It was an extremely hard time for us partly because we didn't understand why and because we wanted a baby *now!* Some of our closest friends and family members continued to pray for us, but Christy and I had just about given up.

CHAPTER FIVE

One day, after 8 ½ years of heartache, I heard God speak to my spirit. He said, "I have called this baby for an appointed time." It was amazing! I know exactly where I was when I heard Him, and I was so excited that I couldn't wait to get back home to tell Christy! When I did, she didn't share the same excitement. She just glared at me with that "I-can't-believe-you're-telling-me-this" look. She had been so disappointed month after month of not being able to have a child that she could not think about the possibility. She couldn't get her hopes up again, just to have them squashed…again. I didn't say much about it, but I felt as if we had renewed hope as I held on to this divine encounter.

Well, about six months later, Christy called and asked me to come home as soon as possible after work. This was in October of 1999, fourteen years after we were married. As I walked through the door, I saw balloons and a card that read "Daddy" and Christy told me she was pregnant! We hugged and cried and praised God for His goodness. You see, God's plan *was* for us to have a baby, but He showed us that *His timing* was different than ours. So, this is the lesson we learned: We can be in His will and praying for something we believe He wants us to have, but also, we must realize it will be delivered in His time and not ours.

"*Forgive us of our sins, as we forgive those who sin against us.*" Here we are asking for God's forgiveness. Yes, we are forgiven when we ask Jesus to come into our hearts, but we are still human, therefore, constantly battling sin in our daily lives. With this passage of the prayer, we are clearing the air, acknowledging we are not perfect and that we need His continued forgiveness.

In the second part of this sentence, we are acknowledging that we are forgiving anyone who has wronged us. If we are carrying a grudge against someone, this is where we ask Him to help us forgive that person. This is very difficult for some people and understandably so. Many people have been abused by others or have lost loved ones in terrible tragedies. If this is you, I can't imagine the hurt you must feel. Life is not fair and never will be, but God asks us to forgive others as He has forgiven us. He goes on to say in Matthew 6:15 and Mark 11:26 that we *must* forgive others or we ourselves will not be forgiven. Forgiveness for many is a tough thing to ask, but God requires us to do it.

"Lead us not into temptation, but deliver us from evil" means to help us as the devil tempts us. God will not lead us into temptation, but the devil will. We need to shun temptation when it comes our way. In this passage of scripture, we are asking God to strengthen us as we are tempted so we can avoid the dangers of sin altogether. Temptation is inevitable, but God provides the escape for us. It starts with conviction in our hearts. Conviction is the crossroads or the decision point. We are either going to choose to heed the call of the Holy Spirit or we are going to partake in the activity we know is wrong.

The closer our walk with Jesus, the easier it is to make the right choice.

"For yours is the kingdom, the power and the glory forever, Amen." This part of the Lord's Prayer sums up our acknowledgment of who God is, how powerful He is and that we know He will reign in glory forever in our hearts and in

CHAPTER FIVE

heaven. (This phrase is not in all manuscripts of the Bible). The Lord's Prayer begins with praise to Him and ends in praise to Him. How fitting for the One who created us and the universe!

Drink from Good Books, Especially the Bible

There are millions of good books in the world. Just pick your internet search topic and you will find so many choices. I like reading books that offer good advice. I want to improve things in my life, so I can make a difference for others. My goals are to be a better husband and father, to be a better leader at the bank, and to be a better friend and mentor. I also desire to be better in the ministry God has given me for the season I'm in. Many people enjoy reading to pass the time. I enjoy reading to improve my life and enjoy writing to help others. I hope this book helps you fulfill the destiny God has for you.

The Bible is God's word. It was written by God through His disciples, prophets, and wise men and women who followed and listened to Him. No, God didn't physically write the Bible, but He gave the words to those who did. The Bible is how we learn about God and His plan for us and the world. By reading, we build our knowledge of God, and through this, our faith is built in Him. You may be asking, "Why do I need to know God and have faith in Him?" You have a purpose in life. God has given you talents and skills and placed desires in your heart to help you fulfill these purposes. The more time you spend with God, the closer you become to Him and the more pointed you are toward your purpose. You then have a keen sense of what you are supposed to be doing with your life.

The closer you get to God, the more He is able to do through you and for you, and this process builds your faith in Him. He wants you to rely on Him in everything you do, large or small.

Proverbs 3:5-6 says, "Trust in the Lord with all your heart; do not depend on your own understanding. Seek His will in all you do, and He will direct your paths." He wants you to be dependent on Him and trust His ways in every circumstance. When you get to this point, He is able to use you for His service through your purpose or calling. You will be happiest and life will be at its most rewarding level when you are using your talents and skills the way He wants you to.

How to Read the Bible

The legendary basketball coach, John Wooden, said we should "drink from good books, especially the Bible." The Bible is the greatest book ever written. It is estimated that there have been over 8 billion copies of the book sold. There are over 100 million copies of the Bible sold each year! The Bible is our road map for life. Every situation we will face in life is covered in the Bible. Just an interesting note: The most discussed topic in the Bible is…money/possessions. That's right! God knows how much we care about our money and the Bible is full of parables and lessons that teach us about this topic.

If you are new to the Bible, it may be best for you to begin in the gospel books of the New Testament, which consist

CHAPTER FIVE

of Matthew, Mark, Luke, and John. These books begin and end with the life of Jesus. Jesus does most of the speaking in these books, where He generally talks with His disciples (His 12 chosen followers) and the crowds that gathered to hear Him. The book of Acts takes you through the acts or good works of the Apostles, as they went throughout the land spreading the good news about Jesus. The late Billy Graham said the gospel of John is a very good one to begin with followed by Acts. Next, you could read 1 John, 2 John & 3 John, Philippians, and Romans.

Some translations of the Bible are hard to read and understand. I like reading the New Living Translation "Daily Walk" version because it summarizes a few chapters before the day's reading. It gives me some background and explains in layman's terms what is happening in the upcoming chapters. This version of the Bible helps to give me a clear understanding of what is being said.

The "Daily Walk" Bible is also designed for 365 readings (one for each day of the year) to help you read the entire Bible in one year's time. So, if you are a history lover and want to know it all from the beginning, the "Daily Walk" version is a great way to study and learn.

The first book of the Bible is Genesis and begins with God's creation of the world and everything in it, including mankind. Genesis is a fascinating account of the first man and woman, Adam and Eve, and how sin was brought into this world. From there it goes into many history and faith lessons, including Noah and the Ark. Some of the main people after Noah were his descendants, Abraham, Isaac, and Jacob. They would be in the lineage of King David and eventually Jesus Christ.

It is important to know the Old Testament history and how everything fits together but remember what your goal is… to become more like Christ. Ephesians 5: 1-2 says, "Follow God's example in everything you do, because you are his dear children. Live a life filled with love for others, following the example of Christ, who loved you and gave Himself as a sacrifice to take away your sins." The New Testament will walk you through the life of Jesus Christ and what He desires for you.

The Bible is a fascinating book. When God is in your life and you are seeking to know Him better, He will point out new things as you read and reread a passage. You will continue to grow as you find a church home and learn from a pastor who is preaching from God's word.

Going to Church

God has called us to assemble with one another. In Hebrews 10:25 the writer of Hebrews says, "Let us not neglect our meeting together, as some people do, but encourage and warn each other, especially now that the day of His coming back again is drawing near." This means we are to gather with other Christ followers and help each other, to pray with, and encourage one another.

Many people believe they get as much out of sitting at home and watching a sermon on television as they do by attending a local church service. I would have to respectfully disagree. I believe we attend church to hear the message and to

CHAPTER FIVE

be fed the word of God. I also believe He wants us there to help and encourage one another. God's two greatest commandments are for us to love Him (Deuteronomy 5:7) and to love each other (John 13:34).

In Matthew 22: 36-39, when Jesus was asked the question, "Teacher, which is the most important commandment in the law of Moses?" He replied, "You must love the Lord your God with all your heart, all your soul, and all your mind. This is the first and greatest commandment. A second is equally important: Love your neighbor as yourself."

We must look for ways to help our brothers and sisters in Christ. Attending a weekly service gives us the opportunity to bond with others and a chance to grow as we hear God's word.

Final Thoughts

Life is a marathon, not a sprint. I have told many people over the years that it's not necessarily the smartest person who becomes successful, it's the person who does the right things, consistently. Consistency is special. It sounds boring but many people do it well. It truly is a wonderful characteristic of these folks. Consistency means you are willing to commit to doing something day in and day out, that you can be counted on, that you're a dependable person and one who can be trusted. If you consistently get up every morning and go to class or to work, you have a better chance of making good grades or getting a promotion. If you consistently save part of your paycheck every two weeks or every month and do this for a long time, you will be able to amass a large sum of money. If you consistently go to the gym and eat the right foods, you will maintain your weight and your good health. Consistency sounds easy, but it takes hard work and commitment. There is nothing easy about being consistent because it takes effort, and many are not willing to put forth this effort.

Don't try to tackle every area of your life at once. This will overwhelm and discourage you causing you to give up the pursuit. Find one area in your life where you are motivated to begin, possibly your eating habits. Once you have a good handle on this, try a form of exercise. Adding in a little at a time is a much more effective and enjoyable way of changing your

FINAL THOUGHTS

habits.

If you consistently do these things and add other positive changes over time, your journey in life will be much more fulfilling. Your accomplishments and overall health will be better because of the changes and efforts you made.

We are only on this earth for a short period of time and each of us is on his/her own journey. Our lives are an open canvas just waiting for our brush strokes to paint the picture. One of the most wonderful but dangerous gifts God gives us is the gift of making our own choices. Wonderful because one choice can change our entire lives for the better, but less fulfilling or even dangerous if that choice is a bad one.

The five areas that have been discussed in this book consist of basic, fundamental principles which can help you live a more meaningful and productive life. Using these principles can direct you to the choices that will help you through your personal journey. You don't have to implement everything at once. Choose some things you can commit to and master those. Once you get the feeling of success, you will be encouraged to go on. You can't change everything you want overnight; however, by being consistent and committed you will be able to manage these areas in time. Remember, life is a marathon not a sprint.

My Prayer for You

Congratulations on finishing this book. My prayer is for you to take these fundamental principles and apply them to your life. It's no accident this book has found you. I believe God has intervened and given you this information at the exact time needed. He has a plan for your life, and He is willing to help you if you are willing to put forth some effort.

If you are still unsure about how to get started, talk with a person you trust. This person could be a parent, teacher, coach, grandparent, pastor, or another wise individual with whom you have a connection. Ask this person if he/she would become your mentor, or at least help you work through some of the details in this book.

There are many experienced people who would love the chance to discuss these principles with you. There are people in your life who want their lives to matter. They are looking for ways to help others. Make a list of these individuals and make an appointment with one of them. I know you will find this time well spent. I wish you all the best on your life's journey and pray that you find your amazing life!

Special Acknowledgments

There was so much time involved in writing and reviewing this book that it took away time from those who mean so much to me. Thanks to my wife, Christy, who encouraged me to pursue this book and offered many suggestions throughout the process. I am grateful for your love, patience, encouragement, and ability to cheer me on when it wasn't easy for you. Our daughter, Micah, who would check on me every now and then and ask how my book was coming along. Also, thank you for editing Chapter Two and reminding me that "Simplified" is the title of the book. To my dad and mom, Bill and Betty Von Ledford, who first read the rough draft and said how much they liked it. Thank you for the values you instilled in your children and for the unconditional love you gave us. Thanks to Rich, Sara and Jon for the experiences we shared growing up together.

The inspiration of my father-in-law, Ben Calvert, who has written some pieces of his own and my mother-in-law, Barbara, who is a source of constant encouragement and always telling me she can't wait to read it. My sister-in-law, Dawn Calvert, who has spent countless hours editing, and helping me through the different avenues of publishing; this book would have never made it to the finish line without your help. My brother-in-law Dale Calvert, who wrote the foreword; thank you for your entrepreneurial spirit which has inspired me to step outside of my comfort zone and do something different.

SPECIAL ACKNOWLEDGMENTS

Thank you to my brother, Rich Ledford and wife Tarrie, brother and sister-in-law, Wade and Anna Calvert, dear friends Butch and Debbie McCoy, Herb Triplett, Randy Ware, David Duzyk, Ed Stepanchuk, Patrick Lager, David Points, Kelli Wise, Dan Manley, Earl Van Dyke, Rebecca Morton, Mark Maynard, and my Pastor, V.P. Palmer, for your part in this process. Thank you to my publisher Adam VanKirk, of Right Eye Graphics, whose professionalism is evidenced by the production of this book.

Thank you to Jack Whitaker and the late Elmer Whitaker for giving me the chance to develop my banking and leadership skills on a higher level 20 years ago. Thank you to Elmer K. Whitaker for reviewing this book and giving recommendations which have been included in these pages. My Whitaker Bank family has been a big part of my life and I am greatly appreciative of the support given to me over the years and the friendships we've shared.

Last but certainly not least, thank you to my former high school English teacher, Ms. Barbara Lyons, who gave me another lesson in English 101, reminding me that, "When in first person, you must remain in first person throughout the paragraph!" Your teaching guidance and enthusiastic encouragement helped me complete this project. You convinced me that you couldn't wait to see it in print and your stamp of approval and excitement meant the world to me. There are many other friends and family members who offered kind words during this process and your kindness is very much appreciated. May God bless you and your families because of your kindness and the interest you have taken in this journey.

SPECIAL ACKNOWLEDGMENTS

Credits given

www.thecalculatorsite.com
www.financialmentor.com
www.monster.com
www.careersidekick.com
www.resume.com
www.google.com
www.pinterest.com
www.affordablecollegesonline.com
www.collegescholarships.org
www.scholarships.com
www.research.collegeboard.org
www.collegedata.com
www.trade-schools.net
www.thesimpledollar.com
www.zety.com
America Association of Community Colleges: www.aacc.nche.edu/
www.communitycollegereview.com
www.studentdebtrelief.us
www.collegequest.com
www.healthgrades.com
New Living Translation, "The Daily Walk Bible"
Pastor Harry B. Jones, Message "Salvation: As Easy as A-B-C"
Coach John Wooden's "7 Point Creed"
Billy Graham Evangelistic Association: www.billygraham.org

About the Author

A husband, father, banker and former football coach, Mark Ledford has a passion to help people live their lives to the fullest. At the age of 22, Mark began his banking career as a teller rising through the ranks to become President of the same community bank in Mt. Sterling, Kentucky where he and his family continue to make their home today.

Mark, a graduate and former football player at Morehead State University, states that the game played an instrumental part in his development as a person and a leader. Voted captain of his college team by his teammates, he led by example and continues this same philosophy in his career and family today. Mark and his wife Christy, have one daughter, Micah.

ORDERING & PRICING:

If you have enjoyed reading *Simplified Success – 5 Keys to an Amazing Life* and would like to order additional copies, please see quantities, pricing, and contact information below.

Paperback Quantities	Price (Free U.S.A. Shipping)
1 copy	$18.00
2-5 copies	$16.00 each
6-10 copies	$15.00 each
11-25 copies	$14.00 each
26-50 copies	$13.00 each
51-100 copies	$12.00 each

Over 100 – Please email to markledfordbooks@gmail.com for pricing information.

To purchase, please send check, money order, or cashier's check and address to:

Mark Ledford
PO Box 258
Mt. Sterling, KY 40353

or

To pay by credit card or PayPal, please visit www.MarkLedfordBooks.com.

Prices listed are good through December 31, 2022.

For pricing after this date, send email to markledfordbooks@gmail.com or visit www.MarkLedfordBooks.com.

Softback and hardback versions are available for purchase at www.MarkLedfordBooks.com.

Thank you for doing your part to help others!

"Don't forget to do good and to share what you have with those in need, for such sacrifices are very pleasing to God."
Hebrews 13:16 NLT